ARNOLD SCHOENBERG

FUNDAMENTALS OF MUSICAL COMPOSITION

EDITED BY

GERALD STRANG

WITH THE COLLABORATION OF

LEONARD STEIN

KU-533-589

ff

faber and faber

First published in 1967
by Faber and Faber Limited
Bloomsbury House, 74–77 Great Russell Street,
London WC1B 3DA

Printed and bound in the UK by CPI Group (UK), Croydon CRO 4YY

All rights reserved

© Estate of Gertrude Schoenberg, 1967

Gerald Strang is hereby identified as editor of this
work in accordance with Section 77 of the Copyright,
Designs and Patents Act 1988

*This book is sold subject to the condition that is shall not
by way of trade or otherwise, be lent, resold, hired out or
otherwise circulated without the publisher's prior consent in
any form of binding or cover other than that in which it is
published and without a similar condition including this
condition being imposed on the subsequent purchaser*

A CIP record for this book
is available from the British Library

ISBN 978-0-571-19658-6
ISBN 0-571-19658-6

8 10 9 7

CONTENTS

PART II

SMALL FORMS

PART III

LARGE FORMS

INTRODUCTION

THIS present book represents the last of the three large textbooks on music theory and practice planned by Arnold Schoenberg largely as the result of his teachings in the United States. Like the two other books, *Structural Functions of Harmony* (Williams & Norgate, 1954) and *Preliminary Exercises in Counterpoint* (Faber & Faber, 1963), this one was intended for 'the average student of the universities' as well as for the talented student who might become a composer (see Schoenberg's statement in the Appendix). As the author states, it was planned as a book of 'technical matters discussed in a very fundamental way'.

Fundamentals of Musical Composition combines two methods of approach: (1) the analysis of masterworks, with special emphasis on the Beethoven piano sonatas; and (2) practice in the writing of musical forms, both small and large. As a book of analysis it amplifies much in the later chapters of *Structural Functions of Harmony*, particularly Chapter XI, 'Progressions for Various Compositional Purposes'. As a method for *preliminary exercises* in composition it enlarges the material of the syllabus, *Models for Beginners in Composition* (G. Schirmer, Inc., 1942).

In *Fundamentals of Musical Composition*, as in all of his manuals of musical practice dating back to his *Harmonielehre* (Universal Edition, 1911; abridged English translation, *Theory of Harmony*, Philosophical Library, 1948), Schoenberg's main pedagogical approach is not just one of theoretical speculation—although one will always find a basic theoretical foundation underlying his practical advice—but of exposing fundamental technical problems in composition and of showing how they might be solved in a number of ways. Through such an approach the student is encouraged to develop his own critical judgement based on the evaluation of many possibilities.

LEONARD STEIN, 1965

EDITOR'S PREFACE

THE *Fundamentals of Musical Composition* grew out of Schoenberg's work with students of analysis and composition at the University of Southern California and the University of California (Los Angeles). Work on it continued intermittently from 1937 until 1948. At the time of his death most of the text had undergone four more or less complete revisions. During these years hundreds of special examples were written to illustrate the text. In the final version a great many of them were replaced by analyses of illustrations from musical literature, and many others were transferred to *Structural Functions of Harmony*.[1]

Since I had worked with Schoenberg on the book throughout the entire period, Mrs. Schoenberg asked me to assume the task of reconciling the various versions and preparing it for publication. The text was substantially complete up to and including the chapter on 'Rondo Forms'; only revision of the English and elimination of some duplications were necessary. The final chapter was incomplete and required reorganization because much of its content had been anticipated in the earlier chapter on 'The Parts of Larger Forms'.

From the very beginning the book was conceived in English, rather than in Schoenberg's native German. This created many problems of terminology and language structure. He rejected much of the traditional terminology in both languages, choosing, instead, to borrow or invent new terms. For example, a whole hierarchy of terms was developed to differentiate the subdivisions of a piece. *Part* is used non-restrictively as a general term. Other terms, in approximate order of size or complexity, include: *motive, unit, element, phrase, fore-sentence, after-sentence, segment, section* and *division*. These terms are used consistently and their meanings are self-evident. Other special terms are explained in the text. I have chosen to keep some of the flavour of Schoenberg's English construction, when it is expressively effective, even though it may be at variance with the idiomatic.

The aim of this book is to provide a basic text for undergraduate work in composition. Thus the first half is devoted to detailed treatment of the technical problems which face the beginner. It is intended to be thoroughly practical, though each recommendation and each process described has been carefully verified by analysis of the practice of master composers. From this point on, the basic concepts, structures and

[1] Arnold Schoenberg, *Structural Functions of Harmony*. New York: Williams & Norgate, London, 1954.

techniques are integrated by applying them to the traditional instrumental forms, in approximate order of complexity.

Schoenberg was convinced that the student of composition must master thoroughly the traditional techniques and organizational methods, and possess a wide and intimate knowledge of musical literature if he wishes to solve the more difficult problems of contemporary music. In this basic text there is little reference to music since 1900, though the student is encouraged to make full use of the resources available up to that time. Nevertheless, the principles stated here can be readily applied to a variety of styles and to contemporary musical materials. Certain aesthetic essentials, such as clarity of statement, contrast, repetition, balance, variation, elaboration, proportion, connexion, transition—these and many others are applicable regardless of style or idiom.

While primarily a textbook on composition, it will be evident that this volume can be used equally well as a text in musical analysis. As such, it emphasizes the composer's insight into musical organization; it is not a mere vocabulary of formal types. The examples are deliberately chosen to illustrate a wide variety of departures from the fictitious 'norm'. Only acquaintance with a wide range of possibilities gives the student enough freedom to meet the unique problems which each individual composition poses.

To simplify the student's analytical problems and reduce the number of lengthy musical examples, most of the references to musical literature are confined to the Beethoven piano sonatas. The first volume of the sonatas, at least, must be considered a required supplement. In later chapters references are broadened to include works of other composers which are readily available in miniature scores.

It was a privilege and a deeply rewarding educational experience to have worked with Schoenberg over these many years on the preparation of this book. I have tried, in preparing this final version, to secure the clear and faithful presentation of the ideas which grew and matured during his experience with American composition students, ideas which were verified by a broad and intensive study of musical literature. All his life Schoenberg laboured to share with his students his knowledge of music. I hope that through this, his last theoretical work on composition, another generation of students may share his inspiration.

GERALD STRANG, 1965

EXPLANATORY NOTE

ALL citations of musical literature which do not specify the composer refer to works by Beethoven. If the title is not specified the reference is to his piano sonatas. Opus number and movement are specified thus: Op. 2/2–III means Beethoven, Piano Sonata, Opus 2, No. 2, third movement.

Measure numbers are specified from the first accented beat of the passage, even though a preceding upbeat is a part of the phrase.

In numbering measures the first *full measure* is numbered one. Where there are alternative endings the second ending starts with the same measure number as the first ending, with an added subscript, e.g. Op. 2/2–I, in which the first ending contains m. 114–17. The second ending accordingly begins with m. 114a, 115a, 116a and 117a. M. 118–21 complete the second ending. The double bar lies *within* m. 121; hence, the first full measure after the double bar is m. 122.

Keys or tonalities are represented by capital or small letters to indicate major or minor: *a* means a minor key on *A*; *F♯* means a major key on *F♯*. Keys reached by modulation are often paired with the Roman numeral indicating the relation of the tonic chord to that of the principal key: from *C*, modulation might lead to *G* (V), *e* (iii), A♭ (♭VI), *f* (iv), etc.

The Roman numerals representing chords also reflect chord quality: I is major; vi is minor, etc. Substitute, or chromatic, harmonies, are often distinguished from the diatonic equivalent by a bar through the middle: ＩＩＩ means a major chord on the third degree substituted for the diatonic minor chord. This same chord in a different context might be referred to as V of vi, i.e. the dominant normally resolving to vi, as in the key of the relative minor.

The distinction between a transient modulation and chromatic harmony is always tenuous. In general, only firmly established modulations lead to analysis in terms of a different key. However, when a chromatic passage remains temporarily among chords associated with another key, the term *region* is used. Thus a reference to the tonic minor region, or subdominant minor region, indicates temporary use of chords derived from the corresponding key, but without fully establishing the new key by a cadence.[1]

The following abbreviations are used throughout the book:

$$\text{Var(s).} = \text{variation(s)}$$
$$\text{Ex(s).} = \text{example(s)}$$

---

[1] For further explanation of *region* and *modulation*, see Schoenberg, *Structural Functions of Harmony*, Chapter III.

GLOSSARY

Original usage	Equivalent English usage
whole note	semibreve
half note	minim
quarter note	crotchet
eighth note	quaver
tone	note
tonality	key
degree (as V or vii)	chord built on a degree of the scale
measure (m.)	bar
voice-leading (or part-leading)	part-writing
authentic cadence	perfect cadence
deceptive cadence (or progression)	interrupted cadence

PART I

CONSTRUCTION OF THEMES

I

THE CONCEPT OF FORM

THE term *form* is used in several different senses. When used in connexion with *binary, ternary* or *rondo form*, it refers chiefly to the number of parts.[1] The phrase *sonata form* suggests, instead, the size of the parts and the complexity of their interrelationships. In speaking of *minuet, scherzo* and other *dance forms*, one has in mind the metre, tempo and rhythmic characteristics which identify the dance.

Used in the aesthetic sense, form means that a piece is *organized*; i.e. that it consists of elements functioning like those of a living *organism*.

Without organization music would be an amorphous mass, as unintelligible as an essay without punctuation, or as disconnected as a conversation which leaps purposelessly from one subject to another.

The chief requirements for the creation of a comprehensible form are *logic* and *coherence*. The presentation, development and interconnexion of ideas must be based on relationship. Ideas must be differentiated according to their importance and function.

Moreover, one can comprehend only what one can keep in mind. Man's mental limitations prevent him from grasping anything which is too extended. Thus appropriate subdivision facilitates understanding and determines the *form*.

The size and number of parts does not always depend on the size of a piece. Generally, the larger the piece, the greater the number of parts. But sometimes a short piece may have the same number of parts as a longer one, just as a midget has the same number of limbs, the same form, as a giant.

A composer does not, of course, add bit by bit, as a child does in building with wooden blocks. He conceives an entire composition as a spontaneous vision. Then he

---

[1] 'Part' is used in the most general sense to indicate undifferentiated elements, sections or subdivisions of a piece. Other terms will be used later to distinguish parts of various sizes and with different functions.

proceeds, like Michelangelo who chiselled his *Moses* out of the marble without sketches, complete in every detail, thus directly *forming* his material.

No beginner is capable of envisaging a composition in its entirety; hence he must proceed gradually, from the simpler to the more complex. Simplified practice forms, which do not always correspond to art forms, help a student to acquire the sense of form and a knowledge of the essentials of construction. It will be useful to start by building musical blocks and connecting them intelligently.

These musical blocks (*phrases, motives,* etc.) will provide the material for building larger units of various kinds, according to the requirements of the structure. Thus the demands of logic, coherence and comprehensibility can be fulfilled, in relation to the need for contrast, variety and fluency of presentation.

II

THE PHRASE

THE smallest structural unit is the *phrase*, a kind of musical molecule consisting of a number of integrated musical events, possessing a certain completeness, and well adapted to combination with other similar units.

The term *phrase* means, structurally, a unit approximating to what one could sing in a single breath (Ex. 1).[1] Its ending suggests a form of punctuation such as a comma. Often some features appear more than once within the phrase. Such 'motivic' characteristics will be discussed in the following chapter.

In homophonic-harmonic music, the essential content is concentrated in one voice, the principal voice, which implies an inherent harmony. The mutual accommodation of melody and harmony is difficult at first. But the composer should never invent a melody without being conscious of its harmony.

When the melodic idea consists entirely or largely of notes outlining a single harmony, or a simple succession of harmonies, there is little difficulty in determining and expressing the harmonic implications. With such a clear harmonic skeleton, even rather elaborate melodic ideas can be readily related to their inherent harmony. Exs. 2 and 3 illustrate such cases at several levels. Almost any simple harmonic progression can be used, but for opening phrases I and V are especially useful, since they express the key most clearly.

The addition of non-chordal notes contributes to the fluency and interest of the phrase, provided they do not obscure or contradict the harmony. The various 'conventional formulas' for using non-chordal notes (passing notes, auxiliary notes, changing notes, suspensions, appoggiaturas, etc.) provide for harmonic clarity through the resolution of non-chordal into chordal notes.

Rhythm is particularly important in moulding the phrase. It contributes to interest and variety; it establishes character; and it is often the determining factor in establishing the unity of the phrase. The end of the phrase is usually differentiated rhythmically to provide punctuation.

Phrase endings may be marked by a combination of distinguishing features, such as rhythmic reduction, melodic relaxation through a drop in pitch, the use of smaller intervals and fewer notes; or by any other suitable differentiation.

The length of a phrase may vary within wide limits (Ex. 4). Metre and tempo have a great deal to do with phrase-length. In compound metres a length of two measures

[1] Exs. 1-11 at end of chapter, pp. 5-7.

may be considered the average; in simple metres a length of four measures is normal. But in very slow tempos the phrase may be reduced to half a measure; and in very rapid tempos eight measures or more may constitute a single phrase.

The phrase is seldom an exact multiple of the measure length; it usually varies by a beat or more. And nearly always the phrase crosses the metrical subdivisions, rather than filling the measures completely.

There is no intrinsic reason for a phrase to be restricted to an even number. But the consequences of irregularity are so far reaching that discussion of such cases will be reserved for Chapter XIV.

COMMENT ON EXAMPLES[1]

In the early stages a composer's invention seldom flows freely. The control of melodic, rhythmic and harmonic factors impedes the spontaneous conception of musical ideas. It is possible to stimulate the inventive faculties and acquire technical facility by making a great many sketches of phrases based on a predetermined harmony. At first, such attempts may be stiff and awkward, but, with patience, the co-ordination of the various elements will rapidly become smoother, until real fluency and even expressiveness is attained.

Exs. 5–11 may be taken as an outline for practise. Here a single harmony, the tonic of *F* major, is taken as a basis. Ex. 5 shows a few of the contours which can be created by various arrangements of the notes of the chord. In Ex. 6 smaller note-values produce different results. Ex. 7, still confined to notes of the chord, illustrates the variety that can be achieved by combining different note-values (study also Exs. 2*d, e, h*).

Exs. 8 and 9, based on Exs. 5 and 7, show how the simplest melodic and rhythmic additions can contribute fluency and vitality (study also Exs. 2 and 3).

The more elaborate embellishments of Exs. 10 and 11 contribute flexibility and richness of detail, but tend to overburden the melody with small notes and obscure the harmony.

---

[1] The examples will come at the ends of chapters following the 'Comment on Examples'.

Ex. 1

Ex. 2

Ex. 3

Ex.8
Varying Ex.5 by adding passing notes

Ex.9
Varying Ex.7 by adding passing notes and note repetitions

Ex.10
Embellishing Ex.8

Ex.11
Varying Ex.7 by using appoggiaturas and changing notes

III

THE MOTIVE

EVEN the writing of simple phrases involves the invention and use of motives, though perhaps unconsciously. Consciously used, the motive should produce unity, relationship, coherence, logic, comprehensibility and fluency.

The *motive* generally appears in a characteristic and impressive manner at the beginning of a piece. The features of a motive are intervals and rhythms, combined to produce a memorable shape or contour which usually implies an inherent harmony. Inasmuch as almost every figure within a piece reveals some relationship to it, the basic motive is often considered the 'germ' of the idea. Since it includes elements, at least, of every subsequent musical figure, one could consider it the 'smallest common multiple'. And since it is included in every subsequent figure, it could be considered the 'greatest common factor'.

However, everything depends on its use. Whether a motive be simple or complex, whether it consists of few or many features, the final impression of the piece is not determined by its primary form. Everything depends on its treatment and development.

A motive appears constantly throughout a piece: *it is repeated*. Repetition alone often gives rise to *monotony*. Monotony can only be overcome by *variation*.

Use of the motive requires variation

Variation means change. But changing every feature produces something foreign, incoherent, illogical. It destroys the basic shape of the motive.

Accordingly, variation requires changing some of the less-important features and preserving some of the more-important ones. Preservation of rhythmic features effectively produces coherence (though monotony cannot be avoided without slight changes). For the rest, determining which features are more important depends on the compositional objective. Through substantial changes, a variety of *motive-forms*, adapted to every formal function, can be produced.

Homophonic music can be called the style of 'developing variation'. This means that in the succession of motive-forms produced through variation of the basic motive, there is something which can be compared to development, to growth. But changes of subordinate meaning, which have no special consequences, have only the local effect of an embellishment. Such changes are better termed *variants*.

WHAT CONSTITUTES A MOTIVE

Any rhythmicized succession of notes can be used as a basic motive, but there should not be too many different features.

Rhythmic features may be very simple, even for the main theme of a sonata (Ex. 12*a*). A symphony can be built on scarcely more complex rhythmic features (Exs. 12*b*, *c*, 13). The examples from Beethoven's Fifth symphony consist primarily of note-repetitions, which sometimes contribute distinctive characteristics.

A motive need not contain a great many interval features. The main theme of Brahms's Fourth symphony (Ex. 13), though also containing sixths and octaves, is, as the analysis shows, constructed on a succession of thirds.

Often a contour or shape is significant, although the rhythmic treatment and intervals change. The upward leap in Ex. 12*a*; the movement up by step in Ex. 16; the upward sweep followed by a return within it which pervades Beethoven's Op. 2/3–IV,[1] illustrate such cases.

Every element or feature of a motive or phrase must be considered to be a motive if it is treated as such, i.e. if it is repeated with or without variation.

TREATMENT AND UTILIZATION OF THE MOTIVE

A motive is used by repetition. The repetition may be exact, modified or developed.

Exact repetitions preserve all features and relationships. Transpositions to a different degree, inversions, retrogrades, diminutions and augmentations are exact repetitions if they preserve strictly the features and note relations (Ex. 14).

Modified repetitions are created through variation. They provide variety and produce new material (motive-forms) for subsequent use.

Some variations, however, are merely local 'variants' and have little or no influence on the continuation.

Variation, it must be remembered, is repetition in which some features are changed and the rest preserved.

All the features of rhythm, interval, harmony and contour are subject to various alterations. Frequently, several methods of variation are applied to several features simultaneously; but such changes must not produce a motive-form too foreign to the basic motive. In the course of a piece, a motive-form may be developed further through subsequent variation. Exs. 15 and 16 are illustrations.

COMMENT ON EXAMPLES

In Exs. 17–29, based solely on a broken chord, some of the methods which can be applied are shown as systematically as is practicable.

---

[1] References to the literature identified only by opus number apply to Beethoven piano sonatas. Because of their general accessibility, a great many references to them appear in the later chapters.

The *rhythm* is changed:

1. By modifying the length of the notes (Ex. 17).
2. By note repetitions (Exs. 17*h*, *i*, *k*, *l*, *n*).
3. By repetition of certain rhythms (Exs. 17*l*, *m*, 18*e*).
4. By shifting rhythms to different beats (Ex. 23; in particular, compare 23*d* with 23*e*, *f*, *g*).
5. By addition of upbeats (Ex. 22).
6. By changing the metre—a device seldom usable within a piece (Ex. 24).

The *intervals* are changed:

1. By changing the original order or direction of the notes (Ex. 19).
2. By addition or omission of intervals (Ex. 21).
3. By filling up intervals with ancillary[1] notes (Exs. 18, 20 ff.).
4. By reduction through omission or condensation (Ex. 21).
5. By repetition of features (Exs. 20*h*, 22*a*, *b*, *d*).
6. By shifting features to other beats (Ex. 23).

The *harmony* is changed:

1. By the use of inversions (Exs. 25*a*, *b*).
2. By additions at the end (Exs. 25 *c–i*).
3. By insertions in the middle (Ex. 26).
4. By substituting a different chord (Exs. 27*a*, *b*, *c*) or succession (Exs. 27*d–i*).

The *melody* is adapted to these changes:

1. By transposition (Ex. 28).
2. By addition of passing harmonies (Ex. 29).
3. By 'semi-contrapuntal' treatment of the accompaniment (Ex. 29).

Such exploration of the resources of variation can be of great assistance in the acquisition of technical skill and the development of a rich inventive faculty.

---

[1] In order to avoid aesthetically misleading and corrupted terms, *ancillary* will be preferred in referring to the so-called 'embellishing' or 'ornamental' notes of conventional melodic formulas.

Ex.16

b) Op.22-III

Ex.17

Developing variations of a motive based on a broken chord

Rhythmic changes

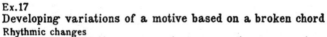

Ex.18

Addition of ancillary notes

Ex.19

Changing the original order

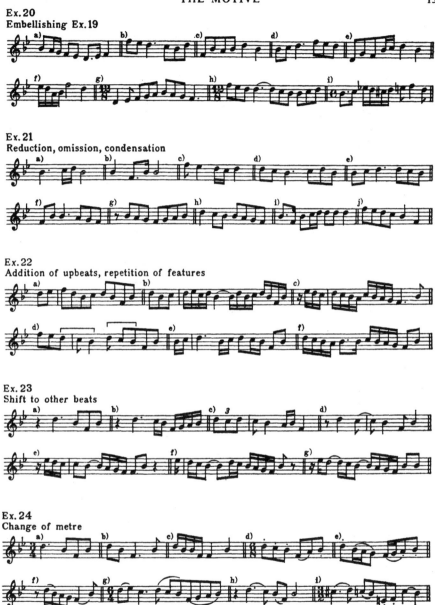

Ex. 20
Embellishing Ex. 19

Ex. 21
Reduction, omission, condensation

Ex. 22
Addition of upbeats, repetition of features

Ex. 23
Shift to other beats

Ex. 24
Change of metre

Ex. 25
Adaptation to richer harmony (cf. Ex. 21d)

Ex. 26

IV

CONNECTING MOTIVE-FORMS

ARTISTICALLY, the connexion of motive-forms depends on factors which can only be discussed at a later stage. However, the mechanics of combination can be described and demonstrated, while temporarily disregarding the stiffness of some of the resulting phrases.

Common content, rhythmic similarities and coherent harmony contribute to logic. Common content is provided by using motive-forms derived from the same basic motive. Rhythmic similarities act as unifying elements. Coherent harmony[1] reinforces relationship.

In a general way every piece of music resembles a cadence, of which each phrase will be a more or less elaborate part. In simple cases a mere interchange of I–V–I, if not contradicted by controversial harmonies, can express a tonality. As used in traditional music, such an interchange is generally concluded with a more elaborate cadence.[2]

Ordinarily the harmony moves more slowly than the melody; in other words, a number of melodic notes usually refers to a single harmony (Exs. 43, 44, 45, 58, etc.).[3] The contrary occasionally occurs when the harmony moves quasi-contrapuntally against a melody in long notes (Exs. 51c, m. 17, 58g). Naturally, the accompanying harmony should reveal a certain regularity. As *motive of the harmony* and *motive of the accompaniment*, through motive-like repetitions, this regularity contributes to unity and comprehensibility (Chapter IX).

A well-balanced melody progresses in waves, i.e. each elevation is countered by a depression. It approaches a high point or climax through a series of intermediate lesser high points, interrupted by recessions. Upward movements are balanced by downward movements; large intervals are compensated for by conjunct movement in the opposite direction. A good melody generally remains within a reasonable compass, not straying too far from a central range.

BUILDING PHRASES

Exs. 30–34 show various methods of producing a large number of different phrases out of one basic motive. Some of them might be used to begin a theme, others to

---

[1] The concept of coherent harmony used here is deduced from the practice of the period from Bach to Wagner.

[2] For evaluation and explanation of the 'root progressions', see Arnold Schoenberg, *Theory of Harmony*, pp. 70 ff., and *Structural Functions of Harmony*, Chapter II.

[3] Exs. 42–51 at end of Chapter VII; Exs. 52–61 at end of Chapter VIII.

continue it; and some, especially those which do not begin with I, as material to meet other structural requirements, e.g. contrasts, subordinate ideas and the like. Motivic features are indicated by brackets and letters. A detailed analysis will reveal many additional relationships to the basic motive.

In Ex. 31 the original form is varied by adding ancillary notes, though all notes of the basic motive are retained. In Ex. 32 the rhythm is preserved, producing closely related motive-forms in spite of changes in interval and direction. Combined with transpositions to other degrees, this procedure is often used in traditional music to produce entire themes (see, for example, Ex. 52). In such cases each note of the melody is either a harmony note or a non-chordal note that corresponds to one of the established conventional formulas.

In Ex. 33 more far-reaching variations are produced by combining rhythmic changes with the addition of ancillary notes, as well as with changes of interval and direction. Even though some of the examples are rather stiff and overcrowded, the practice of making such sketches, which attempt various methods of variation, should never be abandoned.

Other far-reaching variations are shown in Ex. 34. Through such rhythmic shifting and rearrangement of features, material is produced for the continuation of extended themes, and for contrasts. But the use of such remotely related motive-forms may endanger comprehensibility.

In working out derivatives of a motive, it is important that the results have the character of true phrases—of complete musical *units*.

Ex. 30

A phrase built from a broken-chord derivative (Ex. 21d)

Ex. 31

Closely related motive-forms; essential rhythmic features retained

Ex. 32

Rhythm strictly preserved; changes of direction and transposition

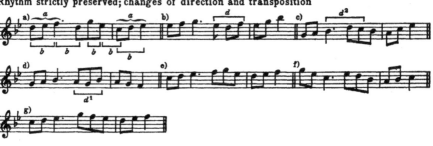

Ex. 33

Ex. 34
Rhythmic shifts, added upbeats, reduction, omission of features

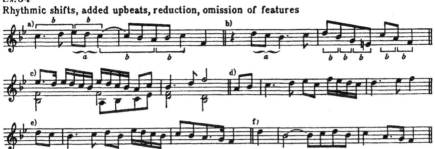

V

CONSTRUCTION OF SIMPLE THEMES

1. BEGINNING THE SENTENCE

IN the first chapter, 'The Concept of Form', it was stated that a piece of music consists of a number of parts. They differ more or less in content, character and mood; in tonality, size and structure. These differences permit presentation of an idea from various viewpoints, producing those contrasts on which variety is based.

Variety must never endanger comprehensibility or logic. Comprehensibility requires limitation of variety, especially if notes, harmonies, motive-forms or contrasts follow each other in rapid succession. Rapidity obstructs one's grasp of an idea. Thus pieces in rapid tempo exhibit a lesser degree of variety.

There are means by which the tendency toward too rapid development, which is often the consequence of disproportionate variety, can be controlled. Delimitation, subdivision and simple repetition are the most useful.

Intelligibility in music seems to be impossible without repetition. While repetition without variation can easily produce monotony, juxtaposition of distantly related elements can easily degenerate into nonsense, especially if unifying elements are omitted. Only so much variation as character, length and tempo required should be admitted: the coherence of motive-forms should be emphasized.

Discretion is especially necessary when the goal is an immediate intelligibility, as in popular music. However, such discretion is not restricted to popular music alone. On the contrary, it is most characteristic of the manner in which the classical masters constructed their forms. They sought a 'popular touch' in their themes, this being the slogan under which the 'ars nova' of the eighteenth century detached itself from the shackles of the contrapuntal style. (Thus, Romain Rolland, in his *Musical Journey*, quotes the German theorist, Mattheson, in his *Vollkommener Kappelmeister* (1739) as saying that in the 'new style' composers *hide* the fact that they write great music. 'A theme should have a certain something which the whole world already knows.')

THE PERIOD AND THE SENTENCE

A complete musical idea or theme is customarily articulated as a period or a sentence. These structures usually appear in classical music as parts of larger forms (e.g. as A in the ABA[1] form), but occasionally are independent (e.g. in strophic songs). There are many different types which are similar in two respects: they centre around a tonic, and they have a definite ending.

In the simplest cases these structures consist of an even number of measures, usually eight or a multiple of eight (i.e. 16 or, in very rapid tempos, even 32, where two or four measures are, in effect, equal to the content of one).

The distinction between the sentence and the period lies in the treatment of the second phrase, and in the continuation after it.

THE BEGINNING OF THE SENTENCE

The construction of the beginning determines the construction of the continuation. In its opening segment a theme must clearly present (in addition to tonality, tempo and metre) its basic motive. The continuation must meet the requirements of comprehensibility. An immediate repetition is the simplest solution, and is characteristic of the sentence structure.

If the beginning is a two-measure phrase, the continuation (m. 3 and 4) may be either an unvaried or a transposed repetition. Slight changes in the melody or harmony may be made without obscuring the repetition.

Illustrations from the literature[1]

In Exs. 58*d*, 59*f* and 60*c*, simple repetition appears with little or no change whatsoever. In Exs. 58*e* and *g*, although the harmony remains the same, the accompaniment is slightly varied and the melody transposed. In Ex. 58*i* the lower octave is used. In Exs. 59*d* and *g* the melody only is slightly varied. In Ex. 61*c* the second measure of the second phrase ascends in conformity with the progress of the harmony towards III. Ex. 53*a* presents an otherwise unvaried transposition to III (the relative major), i.e. a sequence. Ex. 57*a* is sequential in the melody and partially sequential in the accompaniment.

THE DOMINANT FORM: THE COMPLEMENTARY REPETITION[2]

In many classical examples one finds a relationship between first and second phrase similar to that of *dux* (tonic form) and *comes* (dominant form) in the fugue. This kind of repetition, through its slightly contrasting formulation, provides variety in unity.

In the repetition, the rhythm and contour of the melody are preserved. An element of contrast enters through the changed harmony and the necessary adaptation of the melody.

In practising this type of continuation the tonic form may be based on: I, I–V, I–V–I, I–IV or possibly I–II. In these simple cases the dominant form will contrast with the tonic form in the following manner:

[1] Exs. 52–61 at end of Chapter VIII, pp. 63–81.

[2] This is one of many examples of the difficulties associated with loose terminology. *Tonic version* and *dominant version* would be clearer and more precise, but Schoenberg preferred to use the more familiar terms (Ed.).

Tonic form	*Dominant form*
I	V
I–V	V–I
I–V–I	V–I–V
I–IV	V–I
I–II	V–I

In the last two cases, simple reversal of the harmonies is not impossible; but the V–I progression is preferable because it expresses the tonality more clearly. The ending on I preceded by V is so useful that it is often applied when, for example, tonic form is I–II, I–VI or even I–III.

Illustrations from the literature

In Exs. 35a, b and 53b, the first phrase employs only I and the second phrase only V.

The scheme I–V (tonic form), V–I (dominant form) can be observed in Exs. 52b and c. Compare also, among Beethoven's works, the Piano Sonata, Op. 31/2–III (four-measure phrases); and the String Quartets, Op. 59/2–III and Op. 131–IV. The melody is modified only enough to conform with the harmony.

The tonic form of Ex. 36 is based on I–V–I; the dominant form on V–I–V. In Ex. 37 the dominant form includes some passing harmonies. In contrast, the passing harmonies in the tonic form of Ex. 38 are not mechanically preserved in the dominant form. But in Ex. 39, where the tonic form consists of I–IV, the dominant form consists basically of V–I, though more elaborate part-writing disguises it.

COMMENT ON EXAMPLES

The tonic form (m. 1–2) of Ex. 40a is followed (m. 3–4) by a dominant form in which the melody follows the contour of the first phrase exactly. In Exs. 40b and c other dominant forms are shown in which, while the rhythm is preserved, the contour is treated more freely.

In Ex. 41 the dominant forms are varied more than the harmonic change requires. In Exs. 41b and c the tonic form is based on four harmonies, which makes a true answer difficult. To answer literally a tonic form with too many harmonies is impracticable. Here, only the main harmonies, I–V, could be answered, with V–I.

It should be observed that even in these short passages, a definite and regular accompaniment is employed to animate the harmony and to express a specific character. Consistency in the application of accompanimental characteristics is a powerful unifying factor.

Ex. 35
a) Op.2/1-I

b) Op.10/2-I

Ex. 36
Beethoven, String Quartet, Op.18/4-I, m.34-37

Ex. 37
Beethoven, String Quartet, Op.18/6-IV, m.45-48

Ex. 38
Mozart, String Quartet, (K.V. 464)-I

Ex. 39
Mozart, String Quartet, (K.V. 465)-I, m.23-26

Ex. 40
(From Ex. 30)

VI

CONSTRUCTION OF SIMPLE THEMES

2. ANTECEDENT OF THE PERIOD

ONLY a small percentage of all classical themes can be classified as periods. Romantic composers make still less use of them. However, the practise of writing periods is a convenient way to become acquainted with many technical problems.

The construction of the beginning determines the construction of the continuation. The period differs from the sentence in postponement of the repetition. The first phrase is not repeated immediately, but united with more remote (contrasting) motive-forms, to constitute the first half of the period, the *antecedent*. After this contrast repetition cannot be longer postponed without endangering comprehensibility.[1] Thus the second half, the *consequent*, is constructed as a kind of repetition of the antecedent.

In composing periods a practice form will be useful. It should consist of eight measures, divided into an antecedent and consequent of four measures each by a *caesura* in the fourth measure. This caesura, a type of musical punctuation comparable to a comma or semicolon, is carried out in both melody and harmony.

In a great majority of cases the antecedent ends on V, usually approached through a half or full cadence, but sometimes through mere interchange of I and V. Antecedents which end on I also exist.

The consequent usually ends on I, V or III (major or minor) with a full cadence. Although the consequent should be in part a repetition of the antecedent, the cadence, at least, will have to be different, even if it leads to the same degree. Generally, one or two measures of the beginning will be retained, sometimes with more or less variation.

ANALYSIS OF PERIODS FROM BEETHOVEN'S PIANO SONATAS

Op. 2/1-II, Adagio. The antecedent ends on V (m. 4); the consequent on I (m. 8). The harmony of the antecedent is a mere interchange of I and V; the consequent ends

---

[1] The real purpose of musical construction is not beauty, but intelligibility. Former theorists and aestheticians called such forms as the period symmetrical. The term symmetry has probably been applied to music by analogy to the forms of the graphic arts and architecture. But the only really symmetrical forms in music are the mirror forms, derived from contrapuntal music. Real symmetry is not a principle of musical construction. Even if the consequent in a period repeats the antecedent strictly, the structure can only be called 'quasi-symmetrical'. Though quasi-symmetrical construction is used extensively in popular music, that beauty can exist without symmetry is proved by a great many cases of asymmetrical construction.

with a full cadence. The upbeat, which is twice varied, and the feminine ending[1] in m. 2, 4 and 8 are unifying characteristics of this melody. It is significant that the melodic approach to a climax in m. 6 is supported by more frequent changes of the harmony and the increasing use of small notes. The downward movement after the climax is also significant.

Op. 2/2–IV. The caesura on V is reinforced by a half cadence in m. 4. Observe the contrast between the first and second phrases. The consequent deviates harmonically in m. 6, ending with a full cadence on V (m. 8), as if in the key of the dominant. M. 7 and 8, through remote variation and richer movement, produce the necessary intensification of the cadence.

Op. 10/3, Menuetto. The antecedent and consequent consist of eight measures each. In the first four measures of the consequent, the melody and harmony of the antecedent are transposed a note higher, without any other variation.

Op. 10/3, Rondo. This period consists of nine measures, the irregularity resulting from the five measure consequent. The contrast in m. 3–4 makes use of a special device, a chain-like construction. Ex. 42a[2] shows that the end of each motive-form is the beginning of the next; they overlap like the links of a chain. The consequent introduces (m. 5–6) two sequences of the motive, in place of the single repetition in m. 1–2 (Ex. 42b). A premature ending in the seventh measure is evaded through a deceptive cadence, and completed with a varied repetition ending in m. 9.

ANALYSIS OF OTHER ILLUSTRATIONS FROM THE LITERATURE

In Ex. 43 Bach's contrapuntal movement often conceals the caesura. But the period-like repetition of motive-forms is evident. While one of the examples (Ex. 43b) ends on III (the relative major), three others are treated similarly to the Dorian mode; i.e. Exs. 43c and e reach the dominant through a quasi-Phrygian cadence, and Ex. 43d must be classified as having a plagal cadence, though the upper voices, astonishingly, express the authentic cadence. Such a procedure is only justified by the motion of independent parts.

In the Haydn examples, Ex. 44, the caesura (always on V) is sometimes approached through mere interchange, sometimes through half cadences, and occasionally through full cadences. Exs. 44a, e and l are irregular, i.e. they consist of 10, 9 and 9 measures, respectively. The structural meaning of the extensions is indicated. In all the examples m. 3–4 differ significantly from m. 1–2. Even in Ex. 44f, using continuous sixteenth-notes, the figuration and the harmony of m. 3–4 are clearly differentiated. Observe especially the relations and variations marked with brackets.

In some of the Mozart examples, Ex. 45, the repetition at the beginning of the

---

[1] An ending on a strong beat is called 'masculine', and on a weak beat, 'feminine'. Too frequent use of the same kind of ending is often monotonous.

[2] Exs. 42–51 appear at end of Chapter VII, pp. 32–57.

consequent is slightly varied. In Exs. 45*e* and *f*, the inversion of I is used; in Ex. 45*a* the whole consequent is shifted to the lower octave; in Ex. 45*c* the simple doubling of the bass produces an effective variation.

The Beethoven examples, Ex. 46, are chosen principally from the viewpoint of character. In Exs. 46*b*, *d* and *f*, the consequent is built on the dominant. How many variations a single rhythm can undergo is evident in Ex. 46*d*. Note that in both m. 6 and m. 7, two harmonies are used (intensification of the cadence through concentration). In Ex. 46*e* both the antecedent (five measures) and the consequent (seven measures) show remarkable irregularities.

Among the Schubert examples, Ex. 47, two (Exs. 47*b*, *c*) show how beautiful a melody can be built from variations of a single rhythmic figure. Since rhythmic features are more easily remembered than intervallic features, they contribute more effectively to comprehensibility. Constant repetition of a rhythmic figure, as in popular music, lends a popular touch to many Schubertian melodies. But their real nobility manifests itself in their rich melodic contour.

CONSTRUCTION OF THE ANTECEDENT

In the opening section of the sentence, m. 3–4 are constructed as a modified repetition of the first phrase. The antecedent of the period introduces a new problem. Since the consequent is a kind of repetition, the antecedent should be completed with more remote motive-forms in m. 3–4.

As a consequence of the 'tendency of the smallest notes',[1] one may expect an increase in small notes in the continuation of the antecedent. This can be observed in the third (sometimes also in the fourth) measures of Exs. 44*a*, *b*, *c*, *d*, *g*, *k*, 45*a*, *b*, *c*, *d*, *j* and 46*e*.

But the increase of small notes is only one way of constructing m. 3–4 as a contrasting, yet coherent, continuation of m. 1–2. In Exs. 44*f*, *h*, *i*, *j*, *l*, 45*f*, 46*a*, *d*, *f* and 47*b*, *c*, *d*, *e*, the coherence is more evident than the contrast, which consists merely of a change of register, direction or contour.

A coherent contrast can also be produced through a decrease of smaller notes, in which case the motive-form appears to be a reduction (Exs. 43*a*, 45*i*, 46*g*).

Such a decrease is often used to mark melodically the ending of the antecedent, the caesura. Exs. 44*a*, *d*, *g*, *h*, *i*, 45*b*, 46*e*, *f*, *g* and 47*a*, *d* show this usage. Generally, the caesura is supported by a contrast in the contour, which often descends below the register of the beginning (Exs. 44*c*, *d*, *f*, *k*, 45*g*, *j*, 46*e*, 47*a*). Frequently the caesura is approached by receding from an earlier climactic point, as in Exs. 44*a*, *i*, *j*, *k*, 45*a*, *b*, *c*, *f* and 46*a*, *b*, *e*.

[1] The smallest notes in any segment of a piece, even in a motive or motive-form, have an influence on the continuation which can be compared to the momentum of acceleration in a falling body: the longer the movement lasts, the faster it becomes. Thus, if in the beginning only one sixteenth-note is used, very soon an increasing number will appear, growing often into whole passages of sixteenths. To restrict this tendency of the smallest notes requires special care.

When the coherence between the basic motive-forms and the more remote derivatives in m. 3–4 is not quite obvious, a *connective* may bridge the gap. One of the features, often the upbeat or a preceding motive-form, is used to join them. (Exs. 44*d*, *l*, 45*c*, *d*, *g*, 46*e*, 47*d*). But abrupt juxtaposition of contrasting forms need not necessarily produce imbalance (Ex. 45*a*).

As harmonic basis for an antecedent, one can use progressions like those of Exs. 43 to 51. Movement of the harmony in equal notes (i.e. regular change of the harmony) supports unity because it is a primitive kind of 'motive of the accompaniment'.

It should not be forgotten that one purpose of constructing motive-forms from a broken chord (Exs. 5–11, 17–29) was to assure a sound relationship between melody and harmony. To make many sketches of motive-forms, built from broken chords by variation, remains a valuable method of deriving well co-ordinated materials.

One may acquiesce to the 'tendency of the smallest notes'. But too many small notes may produce a crowded effect. On the other hand, in masterpieces one meets cases like the extreme rhythmical contrast between first and second phrases in Exs. 45*a* and *d*. In other Mozart examples (Exs. 45*b*, *g*), the co-ordination of the small notes with the harmony, as ancillary notes, is of a perfection which no beginner dare hope for.

Continuous and thorough study of examples from musical literature is essential.

There are many melodies whose compass is very small (see Exs. 45*i*, 50*a*, *b*). Sometimes when the antecedent remains within a fifth (Ex. 47*e*) or a sixth (Ex. 46*d*) the consequent ascends to a climax. But melodies whose compass at the beginning is very broad (Exs. 44*a*, *c*, *d*, 45*a*) are likely to achieve balance by returning to a middle register. All these examples show that much variety can be achieved within a relatively small compass, though the extension of the compass is often a defence against monotony.

Envisioning a definite character helps to stimulate inventiveness. The *accompaniment* makes important contributions to the expression of character. Such features as differentiation between detached and legato notes (Exs. 44*d*, 47*c*, 48*a*, 50*a*, *e*); rests where harmonization is not required (Exs. 35, 38, 44*h*, 46*b*); unharmonized upbeats (Exs. 44*a*, *g*, 45*f*, 46*b*, *d*, etc.); semicontrapuntal treatment of middle voices (Exs. 41*b*, 44*g*, 45*a*, 48*b*, 51*f*); afterbeat harmony (Exs. 44*c*, *d*, 45*d*, 46*d*, 50*e*); and special rhythmic figures (Exs. 46*j*, 47*b*, 49*a*, 50*a*, 51*f*) should be employed from the very beginning.

It is difficult to reconcile a complex accompaniment with good piano style. Writing for the piano should ignore, as much as possible, the existence of the pedal, i.e. everything should be within easy reach of the fingers.

One must beware of (1) imbalance through overcrowding, (2) destruction of the character and (3) obscuration of the harmonic progression. Fluent part-writing in the accompaniment does not endanger the clarity of the harmony. But control of the root progressions is essential.

VII

CONSTRUCTION OF SIMPLE THEMES

3. CONSEQUENT OF THE PERIOD

THE consequent is a modified repetition of the antecedent, made necessary by the remote motive-forms in m. 3–4. If the period is a complete piece (e.g. children's songs) it must end (usually with a perfect authentic cadence) on I. If it is part of a larger form it may end on I, V or III (major or minor).[1]

An unchanged and complete repetition is very rare. Even in the very simple cases of Exs. 50*b*, *c* and *e*, at least the last measure is modified. Usually, the introduction of a full cadence requires earlier changes. In Exs. 45*i*, *k*, 46*a*, *g* and 50*a* the deviation of the harmony occurs in the seventh measure; and in Exs. 44*i* and 47*c*, *e*, in the sixth measure.

Variation of the harmony can start as early as the first measure of the consequent. In Ex. 45*f* the variation consists in the use of inversions of the same harmonies. The consequent may even begin on a different degree. For instance, in the Menuetto of Beethoven's Op. 10/3, m. 9, it starts on II, as a sequence of the antecedent. In Exs. 44*b* and 46*d*, it begins on V. The harmonic variation in m. 5 of Ex. 47*d* is the beginning of an enriched cadence.

MELODIC CONSIDERATIONS: CADENCE CONTOUR

Variety needs no justification. It is a merit in itself. But some variations in the melody are involuntary results of the changed harmonic construction, particularly of the cadence.

In order to exercise the function of a cadence, the melody must assume certain characteristics, producing a special *cadence contour*, which usually contrasts with what precedes it. The melody parallels the changes in the harmony, obeying the tendency of the smallest notes (like an accelerando), or, on the contrary, contradicting the tendency by employing longer notes (like a ritardando).

Increase of smaller note values is more frequent in cadences than decrease. As examples of rhythmic increase, see, in the Beethoven Sonatas: Op. 2/1, Adagio, m.

---

[1] Sometimes major III occurs in a major key. In Beethoven's String Quartet, Op. 131–V, a (Phrygian) half cadence leads to a (major) III. In his String Quartet, Op. 18/5, Variation 4, a full cadence leads to a (minor) iii in m. 8. Ending on minor v, in a minor key, is illustrated in Ex. 46*k*. In two extraordinary cases (the String Quartets, Op. 59/2–III and Op. 132–V), Beethoven even makes use of VII (dominant of relat've major) in minor.

6–7; Op. 2/2–IV, m. 7; Op. 22, Menuetto, m. 7; Ex. 46*g*, m. 7–8. See also Exs. 44*b*, m. 7; 44*i*, m. 7; 47*c*, m. 6–7; 49*a*, m. 7.

An unusual example of rhythmic decrease is shown in Ex. 46*h*, m. 7. Other examples include Exs. 44*j* and 46*i* (very conspicuous). The two cases in Exs. 44*l* and 47*a* are remarkable because, instead of a rhythmic decrease, a 'written-out ritardando' appears as an extension.

The melody in the cadence commonly reduces characteristic features (which demand continuation) to uncharacteristic ones. Illustrations of this can be found in a great many examples. Compare, for instance, m. 7 of Exs. 45*c* and *f* with their respective m. 1–2. In both cases the characteristic intervals are abandoned, or combined in a different order, and in Ex. 45*c* the eighth-note movement stops entirely with the third and fourth beats.

If there is a climax the melody is likely to recede from it, balancing the compass by returning to the middle register. This decline in the cadence contour, combined with concentration of the harmony and the liquidation of motival obligations, can be depended upon to provide effective delimitation of the structure. See, for example, Exs. 45*f*, *g*.

RHYTHMIC CONSIDERATIONS

Since the consequent is a varied repetition of the antecedent, and since variation does not change all the features but preserves some of them, distantly related motive-forms might sound incoherent.

THE PRESERVATION OF THE RHYTHM ALLOWS EXTENSIVE CHANGES IN THE MELODIC CONTOUR.

Thus in Ex. 47*b* the consequent preserves only one rhythm, abandoning for the sake of unity even the slight variations in m. 2 and 4. This rhythmic unification permits far-reaching changes of the melodic contour in slow tempo, and promotes comprehensibility in rapid tempo. See also Exs. 45*a*, *f*, 46*d*, *j*.

COMMENT ON PERIODS BY ROMANTIC COMPOSERS

Some of the classical examples of Exs. 44–47 deviate from the eight-measure construction. Such deviations can also be found among the examples from Mendelssohn (Ex. 48) and Brahms (Ex. 51). To control such divergencies requires special techniques of extension, reduction, etc., whose discussion must be postponed.

These examples show the various manners in which Romantic composers approach thematic construction. The examples from Brahms are especially interesting because of their harmony. They differ from the classic examples in a more prolific exploitation of the multiple meaning of harmonies. Ex. 51*a* is an illustration. In m. 1–6 there appear only a few harmonies belonging diatonically to *f*-minor; but most of them (at *) could be understood as Neapolitan 6th of *c*-minor, an explanation supported by the immediate continuation. The deviation in m. 3 toward E♭ is surprising. While E♭ might be the dominant of the mediant region (relative major), it is actually treated like a tonic on VII. But in m. 7–8 Brahms finally identifies m. 1–2 and 5–6 as pertaining to c-minor, or, more accurately, to the v-region of f-minor.[1]

In Ex. 51c a repetition (m. 17–32), unchanged in melody and harmony, is varied by supplying a quasi-contrapuntal treatment of the accompanying lower voices.

The construction of Exs. 51d and e will be clarified later (Chapter XV). Observe the use of a *pedal point* in Ex. 51d, at the beginning (m. 1–2) and at the end (m. 10–14).

Though the *pedal point* is often used in masterpieces for expressive or pictorial purposes, its real meaning should be a constructive one. In this sense one finds it at the end of a transition or an elaboration, emphasizing the end of a previous modulation and preparing for the reintroduction of the tonic. In such cases the effect of a pedal point should be one of retardation: it holds back the forward progress of the harmony. Another constructive use of such retardation of the harmonic movement is to balance remote motival variation (a method paralleled by the balancing of centrifugal harmony with simpler motival variation). If no such purpose is involved, a pedal point should be avoided. A moving, melodic bass line is always a greater merit.

In Ex. 51f the tendency of the smallest notes accounts for a variant in m. 5. The rhythmic figure 'a' is shifted from the second beat to the first beat. In consequence, an almost continuous flow of eighth-notes prevails.

[1] The rapid development of harmony since the beginning of the nineteenth century has been the great obstacle to the acceptance of every new composer from Schubert on. Frequent deviation from the tonic region into more or less foreign regions seemed to obstruct unity and intelligibility. However, the most advanced mind is still subject to human limitations. Thus composers of this style, instinctively feeling the danger of incoherence, counteracted the tension in one plane (the complex harmony) by simplification in another plane (the motival and rhythmic construction). This perhaps also explains the unvaried repetitions and frequent sequences of Wagner, Bruckner, Debussy, César Franck, Tchaikovsky, Sibelius and many others.

To the contemporaries of Gustav Mahler, Max Reger, Richard Strauss, Maurice Ravel, etc., far-reaching harmony no longer seriously endangered comprehensibility, and today—even popular composers make a living from it!

Ex. 42
Op. 10/3-IV

Ex. 43   PERIODS

a) *J. S. Bach*, English Suite No. 1, Sarabande

b) English Suite No. 3, Gavotte

c) English Suite No. 4, Menuet II

Phrygian Cadence
to V

d) English Suite No. 6, Sarabande

Plagal Cadence
to V

e) English Suite No. 6, Gavotte I

Phrygian Cadence
to V

Ex. 44

a) *Haydn,* String Quartet, Op.54/1

b) String Quartet, Op.54/1-IV

mere interchange of I and V

full cadence

c) String Quartet, Op. 64/4-I

full cadence

d) String Quartet, Op. 64/4-III

Menuetto

half cadence

e) String Quartet, Op. 64/4-II

Adagio

mere interchange

full cadence

f) String Quartet, Op. 64/5-IV

g) String Quartet, Op.74/3-III

h) String Quartet, Op.76/1-I

i) String Quartet, Op.76/1-II

half
cadence

climatic change of
direction

1) String Quartet, Op.76/5-II

extension, written-out ritardando

Ex. 45

a) *Mozart*, Piano Sonata K.V. 279-III

half cadence

episodic insertion

b) Piano Sonata K.V. 281-I

c) Piano Sonata K.V. 281-III
RONDO
Allegro

d) Piano Sonata K.V. 282-III
Allegro

e) Piano Sonata K.V. 283-II
Andante (1 meas. = 2)

f) Piano Sonata K.V. 284-III

h) Piano Sonata K.V. 311-II
Andantino con espressione

i) Piano Sonata K.V. 331-I
Andante grazioso

j) Piano Sonata K.V. 333-III
Allegretto grazioso

Ex. 46

a) *BEETHOVEN* Septet Op.20-IV

Thema con variazione

b) Septet Op.20-V

SCHERZO (2 meas.: 1)

c) Septet Op.20-V

TRIO

d) String **Trio Op.3-II**
(single rhythmic figure in manifold variations)

e) String Trio Op.8

f) String Trio Op.8

SCHERZO

Allegro molto

g) String Trio Op.8

Allegretto alla Polacca

from the same chain

chain

h) Symphony No. 5-II
Andante con moto

i) String Quartet Op.59/1-III

j) String Quartet Op.18/6-III, Scherzo

k) Piano Concerto, Op.37-III

Ex. 47

a) *SCHUBERT*, Piano Sonata Op. 42-I

written out ritardando

b) Piano Sonata Op. 53-II

multiple variations of upbeat

c) Piano Sonata Op.53-IV

Ex. 48

a) *MENDELSSOHN Im Herbst*, Op.9/5

b) *Hirtenlied*, Op.57/2

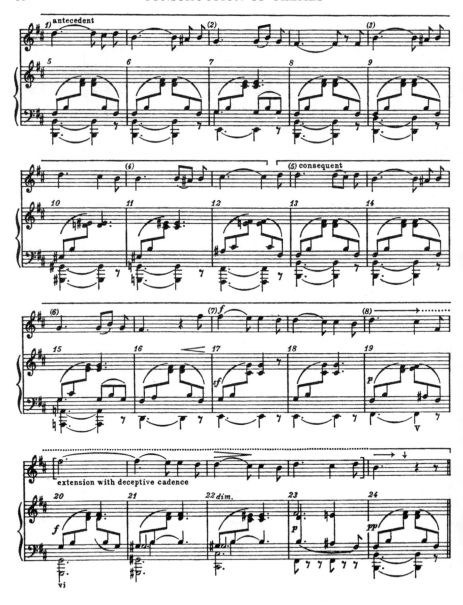

Ex. 49

a) *CHOPIN* Nocturne Op.32/2

b) Nocturne Op.37/1

c) Nocturne Op. 48/1

Ex. 50

a) *SCHUMANN* Album für die Jugend, *Soldatenmarsch*

b) Album für die Jugend, *Trällerliedchen*

c) Album für die Jugend, *Armes Waisenkind*

f) Album für die Jugend, *Sicilianisch*

Ex. 51
a) *BRAHMS* String Quartet Op.51/1-III

c) String Sextet Op.18-IV, Rondo

varied repetition of the period

d) Piano Quartet Op.26-II
Poco Adagio

e) Piano Trio Op.101

Andante grazioso

Period of 6 measures repeated

Andante grazioso

f) Violin Sonata Op.100-II

VIII

CONSTRUCTION OF SIMPLE THEMES

4. COMPLETION OF THE SENTENCE

A PIECE of music resembles in some respects a photograph album, displaying under changing circumstances the life of its basic idea—its basic motive.

The circumstances which produce these various aspects of the basic motive—its variations and developments—derive from considerations of variety, structure, expressiveness, etc.

In contrast to the chronological succession in a photograph album, the order of motive-forms is conditioned by the requirements of comprehensibility and musical logic. Thus, repetition, control of variation, delimitation and subdivision regulate the organization of a piece in its entirety, as well as in its smaller units.

The sentence is a higher form of construction than the period. It not only makes a statement of an idea, but at once starts a kind of development. Since development is the driving force of musical construction, to begin it at once indicates forethought. The sentence form is much used in leading themes of sonatas, symphonies, etc; but it is applicable also to smaller forms.

The beginning of the sentence (Chapter V) already includes repetition; hence, the continuation demands more remotely varied motive-forms. In masterpieces this has given rise to a great variety of structures, some of which will be discussed later. But there are also a great many examples similar to the scheme that will serve as a practice form.

The practice form will consist, in the simpler cases, of eight measures, of which the first four comprise a phrase and its repetition. The technique to be applied in the continuation is a kind of development, comparable in some respects to the condensing technique of 'liquidation'. Development implies not only growth, augmentation, extension and expansion, but also reduction, condensation and intensification. The purpose of liquidation is to counteract the tendency toward unlimited extension.

Liquidation consists in gradually eliminating characteristic features, until only uncharacteristic ones remain, which no longer demand a continuation. Often only residues remain, which have little in common with the basic motive. In conjunction with a cadence or half cadence, this process can be used to provide adequate delimitation for a sentence.

The liquidation is generally supported by a shortening of the phrase. Thus in

Exs. 52*a* and *b*, the two-measure phrases are reduced or condensed[1] (in m. 5–6) to one measure; and in Ex. 52*c*, four measures are condensed to two measures (m. 9–10 and 11–12). This procedure sometimes results in still smaller units: in Ex. 52*b* a half-measure; in Ex. 52*c* one measure.

The end of a sentence calls for the same treatment as the consequent of a period. A sentence may close on I, V or III, with a suitable cadence: full, half, Phrygian, plagal; perfect or imperfect; according to its function.

COMMENT ON EXAMPLES

Exs. 54, 55 and 56 are based on the broken-chord form, Ex. 7*b*. By progressive variation (Exs. 54*a*, *b*, *c*) a motive-form is reached which can be used to build sentences of sharply contrasted character. The endings lead to V and III in major; to v and V in minor. To indicate how easy it is to change the cadence region, even at the very end, alternatives are added for Exs. 56*a* and *b*, ending in the region of the relative major (study also the Trio of Beethoven's Op. 28–III).

Sequence-like procedures[2] are very useful in the continuation of a sentence. The pattern for such sequence treatment is usually a transformation or condensation of preceding motive-forms. Assuming a correct harmonic connexion, the pattern may begin on any degree.

The quasi-sequential repetitions in Exs. 54, 55 and 56 are more or less free transpositions of the pattern a whole- or half-tone up or down, except in Ex. 56*b* where the interval is a fourth down.

[1] Reduction may be accomplished by merely omitting a part of the model. Condensation implies compressing the content of the model, whereby even the order of the features may be somewhat changed.

[2] A *sequence*, in its strictest meaning, *is a repetition* of a segment or unit in its entirety, including the harmony and the accompanying voices, *transposed to another degree*.

A sequence can be executed without using other than diatonic tones; in such cases, the harmony remains 'centripetal', i.e. centred about the tonic region. Diatonic sequences express the tonality clearly and do not endanger balance in the continuation.

When substitutes ('altered' or 'chromatic' chords) are used, the tendency of the harmony may become 'centrifugal'—may produce modulations, to balance which becomes a problem. Substitutes should be used primarily to reinforce the logic of the progression, carefully observing the quasi-melodic function of the substitute tones. For example, a substituted major third tends to lead upward, while a substituted minor third leads down.

The pattern for a sequence must be so built, harmonically and melodically, that it introduces the degree on which the sequence is to begin, and provides a smooth melodic connexion.

Sequences in minor are even more apt to produce modulation than in major, because of the varying forms of the minor scale. In actual practice, sequences in minor are most often built around the natural and descending form; but the strategic reintroduction of the leading-tone is used to prevent premature modulation.

Sequential treatment is not always complete. It may be applied to either melody or harmony alone, the remaining element being more or less freely varied. Such cases may be called *modified* or *partial* sequences. In other cases the general character of a transposed repetition may be present, though without literal transposition of any element. These instances, and others involving variation of some features, may be described as *quasi-sequential*.

The patterns reveal various ways of combining and transforming preceding motive-forms. Only in Exs. 54d and 55b is the order the same as in the first phrase. In Exs. 54e, f, the order is reversed ('b'—'a'). In Ex. 56, only 'b' and 'c' are used. Note that the pattern in Ex. 55a begins with a transposition of that feature which ended the preceding phrase ('c¹', m. 8) and associates it with 'b' in the form used in m. 3 and 7. Observe also the treatment of the motive of the accompaniment, 'e', which (as shown by the analysis in terms of 6/4 metre) is shifted from the weak to the strong measure in m. 9–10.

Illustrations from the literature

Among Exs. 57–61, from Bach, Haydn, Mozart, Schubert and Brahms, there are cases in which the scheme, tonic form—dominant form, is replaced by a different kind of repetition (see Chapter V).

In almost all of these the continuation after the repetition of the first phrase is carried out with condensed phrases giving way to a cadence contour, described in the preceding chapter. Generally these closing measures employ only residues of the basic motive.

As a practice form is only an abstraction from art forms, sentences from master-works often differ considerably from the scheme. Among the illustrations the most obvious deviation lies in the number of measures—there may be either more or less than eight (or multiples of eight). The beginning of Mozart's Overture to *The Marriage of Figaro* (Ex. 59i) is only seven measures.

A length exceeding eight measures is often caused by the use of remote motive-forms, whose establishment demands more than a single repetition; or by the connexion of units of unequal size (e.g. one measure plus two measures); or by insertions.

Ex 53b is such a case. The motive-form in m. 5, though based on the interval of a third, derives indirectly from the figure marked 'b', which could be understood as an embellished syncopation. This is a very remote variation, whose repetitions account for the length of twelve measures.

It is characteristic of Mozart's Rococo technique to produce irregularity within the phrasing through interpolation of incidental repetitions of small segments, residues of a preceding phrase.

In Ex. 59a, after the two one-measure phrases in m. 5 and 6, a segment of three measures (repeated with a slight variation) appears. The example could be reduced to ten measures if m. 10–12 were omitted. Testing which measures could be omitted is the best method to discover what causes the extension. Omitting m. 7–11 would reduce the example to the eight measures of the practice form, indicating that these measures should be considered an insertion, from which the extension results.

In Ex. 59b, m. 5–6 could be omitted.[1]

---

[1] The succession of two 6/4 chords in m. 7 and 9 is most unusual. One might suspect a misprint for such a

In Ex. 59c the omission of m. 7–8 reduces the ten measures to eight.

Ex. 59d is more complicated. The end of this sentence coincides with (overlaps) the beginning of a repetition. Nevertheless, it cannot be considered less than nine measures. The extension is produced by a sequence in m. 6–7.

In Ex. 59h, m. 5–6 are made up of remotely varied motive-forms, because of which a modified repetition follows in m. 7–8. Such extra repetitions are certainly consequences of the requirements of comprehensibility.

The ending (on VI) of Ex. 60a is unusual. Still more unusual is the anticipation of VI (through a deceptive cadence) in m. 10. Were this not the work of a master one would be inclined to call it a weakness. Certainly either of the two alternative versions would be safer for a student. These last four measures make the impression of codettas; if they are, the preceding eight measures might be considered a period. But analysis as a sentence is supported by the similarity of the two segments, m. 1–4 and m. 5–8, to tonic form and dominant form. This hypothesis would lead one to expect a continuation of eight measures.

In Ex. 60c the beginning, on VI–II, is remarkable. The Finale of Beethoven's String Quartet, Op. 130, begins similarly.

In Ex. 60e the (quasi-sequential) repetition of a short segment (m. 7–12) and the condensation in the cadence show a certain similarity to the practice form. Otherwise, the preceding six measures have merely an introductory character.

The first six measures of Ex. 60f consist of two units of three measures each, organized similarly to the tonic- and dominant-form. These three-measure segments are not produced by reduction or extension, but by quasi-sequential insertions, repetitions of m. 2 and 4.[1]

Omitting m. 7–11 and m. 13 would reduce Ex. 60h to the eight measures of the practice form. However, m. 7–14 could also be considered as an independent addition of four measures with a varied repetition. Though 'a₅' is an augmentation of 'a', the phrase in m. 7–8 must be considered a remote variation, justifying the repetition.

The analysis of Ex. 61a shows that the theme is less complicated than it appears at first glance. (The theme or melody need not, of course, always be in the highest voice. Accompaniment and melody may exchange places in various ways. Naturally, the

bass as that indicated below m. 6–7. Such a treatment of a 6/4 chord would scarcely be found elsewhere in Mozart. But since he uses the same 6/4 for a cadence to I (m. 25, 27), one must abandon the idea of a misprint. Misprint or stroke of genius, it is hardly a model for the student to imitate.

[1] Schubert was distinctly one of the pioneers in the field of harmony. The singularity of his harmonic feeling can be observed in the ending of Ex. 60b. As a varied repetition of m. 1–8, m. 9–16 should end on I; but instead the repetition ends on the subdominant! That this is no weakness is evident from the recapitulation, which starts on the subdominant (instead of the tonic) but ends on the tonic, though a strict transposition would have ended on A♭. Thus the harmonic scheme is I–IV : IV–I. If he had used the procedure of the recapitulation in m. 15–16, the cadence would have led in m. 16 to V.

Such discussion is not intended as criticism of the masters, but rather as a warning to the student against harmonic procedures which are beyond his control.

meaning of the harmony must not be obscured, as it might be by misplaced 6/4 chords.)

Ex. 61*b* has little in common with the practice form except for the repetitions of smaller segments (m. 5, 6) and the cadential process, in which the one-measure phrases of m. 3 and 4 are reduced to half-measure residues in m. 7–8, as confirmed by the phrasing in the accompaniment. It has been stated that homophonic music can be called the style of 'developing variation'. Ex. 61*b* is a very clear illustration. The analysis shows that all the motive-forms and phrases of this melody develop gradually out of the first three notes, or perhaps even out of the first two notes.

Ex. 61*d* would be eight measures were it not for the insertion of the motive-form 'b' and its repetition 'b_1' (m. 3). The refrain-like recurrence of the opening phrase in m. 8–9 is remarkable.

All these more complicated structures can be related to the practice form by generalizing the concept on which the practice form was based. The tonic- and dominant-forms (or any comparable twofold statement, even if incomplete) may be considered as the establishment of an idea and of a tonality; thus, the foundation is laid for drawing inferences. In higher art forms, after such an adequate establishment, remotely varied motive-forms may appear at once, without endangering comprehensibility. The appropriate treatment of the remote motive-forms, through varied or sequential repetitions, then justifies irregularity in length, and unusual harmonization.

Applying this generalization to Ex. 57*a*, it becomes apparent that after a twofold statement of a basic phrase, such remote derivatives can be used as appear in m. 5–6. On the other hand, the analysis shows the motival connexion. The extension is produced by the sequence in m. 6.

SENTENCES

Ex. 53

Ex. 54

Ex.56

Ex. 57

BACH- St. Matthew Passion, No.12 ARIE

Ex. 58

a) *HAYDN* Piano Sonata No. 27-II

b) Piano Sonata No. 27-III

c) Piano Sonata No.30-III
Tema con variazioni
Tempo di Menuetto

d) Piano Sonata No.28-I
Allegro moderato

e) Piano Sonata No.33-I
Allegro

f) Piano Sonata No. 41-I
Allegro

g) Piano Sonata No. 41-II
Allegro di molto

h) Piano Sonata No. 34-II
Adagio

i) Piano Sonata No.31-I

Ex.59
a) *MOZART* Piano Sonata K.V. 280-I

b) Piano Sonata K.V. 282-II

c) Piano Sonata K.V. 283-I

f) Piano Sonata K.V. 330-I

Allegro moderato

g) Piano Sonata K.V. 330-III

Allegretto

h) Piano Sonata K.V. 333-I

i) Overture, Marriage of Figaro

Ex.60

a) *SCHUBERT* Piano Sonata Op.122-III

Alternative No.1

Alternative No.2

b) Piano Sonata Op. Post.- III
Scherzo
Allegro vivace con delicatezza

Alternative ending on V

c) Piano Sonata Op. Post.-IV

d) String Quartet, Op. 29-I

e) String Quartet, Op. 29-III

f) String Quartet, Op.125/1-I

g) String Quartet, Op 125/1-II

h) String Quartet, Op.Post.-I

i) String Quartet, Op.161-I

Ex. 61

a) *Brahms,* Cello Sonata Op.38-I

Allegro non troppo

b) Cello Sonata Op. 38-I (m. 58-65)

c) Cello Sonata Op.38-II

d) Violin Sonata Op.78-II

IX

THE ACCOMPANIMENT

THE accompaniment should not be a mere addition. It should be as functional as possible, and at best should act as a complement to the essentials of its subject: the tonality, rhythm, phrasing, contour, character and mood. It should reveal the inherent harmony of the theme, and establishes a unifying motus. It should satisfy the necessities and exploits the resources of the instrument (or group of instruments).

Accompaniment becomes imperative if the harmony or rhythm is complicated. In descriptive music, the accompaniment contributes much to the expressive sonority.

OMISSIBILITY OF THE ACCOMPANIMENT

Of course, unaccompanied music exists, in folk music, ancient church music, solo sonatas for various instruments, etc. Unaccompanied segments often appear in otherwise accompanied music. But even in simple folk music, where the melody requires no harmonic support, an accompaniment (not structurally required) is often added.

Any harmonically self-sufficient melodic segment may remain unaccompanied, supplying contrast and transparency which may contribute to the character of the piece. Transparency is a merit in itself. Moreover, pauses never sound bad!

Upbeats often remain unaccompanied, if there is no question about the harmonic meaning. See, for example, Beethoven, Op. 2/1–II and III; Op. 2/2–III; Op. 7–IV, etc.

Frequently, the beginning segment of a theme is unaccompanied (or in unison). Op. 2/1–I; Op. 10/1–III; Op. 10/2–II; Op. 10/3–I (m. 1–4 and m. 17–22); Op. 26–IV; Op. 28–III;[1] Op. 57–I.

An unaccompanied beginning where the treatment is contrapuntal or semi-contrapuntal is self-explanatory. Op. 2/3–III; Op. 10/2–III.

Unaccompanied figures within a theme also occur. Op. 2/1–I; Op. 10/2–I; Op. 10/3–I, m. 56 ff. and m. 105 ff.

The end of an elaboration is often unaccompanied. Op. 2/2, Rondo, m. 95 ff.; Op. 2/3, Scherzo, m. 37 ff.; Op. 13–I, m. 187 ff. Op. 53, Rondo presents a special case (m. 98 ff.), where the remodulation from the relative minor to tonic is carried out in simple unison.

Though the omission of accompaniment may contribute to transparency, it should

---

[1] A piquant ambiguity. The $f\sharp$ could suggest the keys of $F\sharp$ or B (major or minor). That it implies D is only unmasked in m. 5–8.

be confined to self-explanatory segments. Accompaniment of harmonically ambiguous passages is mandatory.

THE MOTIVE OF THE ACCOMPANIMENT

As a unifying device the accompaniment must be organized in a manner similar to the organization of a theme: by utilization of a motive, the *motive of the accompaniment*.

The motive of the accompaniment can seldom be worked out with as much variety and development as that of a melody, or theme. Its treatment consists, rather, of simple rhythmic repetition, and adaptation to the harmony. Its special form must be so constituted that it can be modified, liquidated or abandoned, as the nature of the theme demands.

TYPES OF ACCOMPANIMENT

Chorale-like. This kind of accompaniment is rather seldom used in instrumental music. One finds it more often in homophonic choral music, in which all the voices sing the same rhythm according to the text, as in the Pilgrim's Chorus from Wagner's *Tannhäuser*, Ex. 62*a*. Some examples from instrumental music are shown in Exs. 62*b*, *c* and *d*. See also Beethoven, Op. 14/2–II; Op. 31/3–III, Trio; Op. 53–I, m. 35 ff.; Op. 78–II; Op. 27/2–II; Ex. 47*b*.

Figuration. The requirements of piano style are better fulfilled through the use of broken chords, although the voice leading remains essentially chorale-like. Compare Ex. 63*a* with Ex. 63*b*, from which it is an extract. As in this case, a broken-chord accompaniment will use one or more special figures systematically—the motive of the accompaniment.

In general the accompaniment makes use of shorter notes than the melody (Exs. 46*e*, 48*d*, 49*a*, 50*b*, 51*d*, 60*b*). However, the contrary also occurs (Ex. 47*c*). There are also innumerable cases like Ex. 45*f*.

The manner in which a figure can be maintained and adapted to the harmony can be seen in Op. 2/1–I, m. 20–21 and 26 ff.; Op. 2/1–II, m. 9 ff. and 37 ff.; Op. 2/2–I, m. 58 ff.; Op. 10/3–II, m. 65 ff.; Op. 10/3–III, Trio, etc. This type of accompaniment is usually not much more than figurated chorale harmony, and may lie in lower, middle or upper voices.

The motive of the accompaniment often includes auxiliaries, appoggiaturas, changing notes, etc. (Op. 2/3–II, m. 11 ff.; Op. 7–IV, m. 64 ff.; Op. 10/2–I, m. 19 ff.). Sometimes it includes a semi-contrapuntal movement of one of the voices (Op. 10/1–I, m. 56 ff.).

The broken chords may of course be distributed in open position (Exs. 49*a*, 64*a*, *b*, *c*). The Romantic style of transcription for piano is illustrated in Ex. 64*d*. The figure in the left hand does not appear in the orchestral score. This technique of making the piano 'roar' was much abused during the nineteenth century.

The method of repeating full chords (Op. 53–I; Exs. 59a, d) is related to the repetition of harmonies in broken-chord style. It derives from the same circumstance: the desire to revive the short-lived tone of the piano.

Sometimes more than one motive of the accompaniment appears, e.g. when the bass, separated from the system of the middle voices, carries out a system of its own (Exs. 64e, f). This procedure is frequently used in combination with rhythmicized chord repetitions (Ex. 65). Occasionally, the bass is systematically placed on a weak beat (Exs. 65q–t).

Intermittent. The harmony may appear only once in a measure, or once in several measures. It may be sustained (Op. 2/3–I, m. 97–108; Ex. 58h); or a short chord may be stated at the beginning of a measure (Op. 10/1–I, m. 1–3; Op. 10/2–I, m. 1–4; Exs. 58c, f); or a short chord may occur during a rest or a sustained note of the melody (Op. 2/2–III, m. 1–2, 5–6; Ex. 46d).

Afterbeat harmony, including syncopations, appears in many forms, e.g. Op. 2/1–I, m. 2–8, 41–46; Op. 2/2, Scherzo; Op. 14/1–I, m. 1–3.

Complementary. Complementary rhythm is that relation between voices or groups of voices in which one voice fills out the gaps in the movement of the others, thus maintaining the motus, i.e. the regular subdivision of the measure. The accompaniment is often added as a complement to the basic rhythm of the principal part (Op. 14/2–I, m. 1–4, 26–27, etc.; Op. 109–I, m. 1–8; Exs. 67a, b; Op. 2/2, Scherzo). There exist many hybrid cases like Op. 10/3–IV, m. 17–22; Op. 31/2–III, especially m. 17–21; Op. 54–I, m. 1–2–5–6. Other cases derive from semi-contrapuntal devices (Exs. 45d, 66a, 67c).

VOICE LEADING

Piano style does not require strict preservation of the number of voices, as in four-part (chorale) harmony. If a piece starts in three or four parts, this number of parts will be used rather consistently. But sometimes fewer voices are used (as if one or more rested) and sometimes more are used (as in the orchestra, when for a crescendo, accentuation, climax or other special effect, additional instruments enter).

If the basic voice-leading is free from parallel octaves, each individual voice can be doubled in octaves, especially if the doubling is consistently maintained, as in Ex. 63. Doubling of the bass can produce variety or contrast through change of register. In Ex. 45g, compare m. 1–2 and 5–6 with 3–4 and 7–8; and in Ex. 46a, compare 5–8 with 1–4. The melody, of course, is often doubled. See, for instance, Exs. 46e and 60e; and Beethoven, Op. 10/1–I, m. 108 ff.; Op. 10/2–I, m. 19 ff.; Op. 14/1–I, m. 61; Op. 26–I, Variation III. Sometimes, even the inner voices are doubled (Exs. 66b, c). Such doubling may appear incidentally for some special effect.

Contrapuntal treatment. A real contrapuntal style appears occasionally, when fugues or fugatos are incorporated in otherwise homophonic music. Sometimes a movement begins with a fugato (Op. 10/2–III; Mozart's String Quartet in *G*, Finale; Beethoven's String Quartet, Op. 59/3, Finale, etc.). Though such sections are often repeated in a more developed form, the remainder should generally be classified as homophonic.

In the elaboration division (development) of larger forms, there are frequently fugato episodes (Beethoven's String Quartet, Op. 59/1–I; first and fourth movements of his *Eroica* Symphony; third movement of Brahms's Piano Quintet; Beethoven, Op. 101, Finale; etc.).

Beethoven (Op. 120, Op. 35) and Brahms (Op. 24) conclude sets of variations with real fugues; and the finales of Beethoven's Sonatas, Op. 106 and Op. 110, are also fugues.

Contrapuntal episodes, generally using imitations or invertible counterpoint, are frequently to be found in elaborations. See Op. 2/3–I, m. 115 ff.; Op. 22, Rondo, m. 81 ff.; Op. 81*a*–I, Coda. The canonic passage beginning the $E\flat$ section of Op. 106–I is unusually long.

Semi- and quasi-contrapuntal treatment. While semi-counterpoint has motival and even thematic implications, quasi-counterpoint is often little more than a way of embellishing, melodizing and vitalizing otherwise unimportant voices in the harmony.

Semi-counterpoint is not based on combinations such as multiple counterpoint, canonic imitations, etc., but only on a free melodic movement of one or more voices, as in Op. 2/2–I, m. 11–16 and the imitations in m. 32 ff.; also Op. 2/3–IV, m. 57 ff.

In real homophonic music there is always one main voice; the addition of imitations, canonic or free, is principally a method of accompanying this main voice. Ostinatos such as, for example, those in Brahms's First Symphony—IV, eight measures after 'E', and in the Finale of the *Variations on a Theme of Haydn*, may be understood similarly. Considering the bass as the main voice, this technique resembles the adding of voices to a 'cantus firmus', constantly varying the texture, as in a passacaglia.

The addition of a countermelody could also be considered a semi-contrapuntal device. See Op. 26–II, m. 45 ff.; Op. 28–I, m. 183 ff. (this passage, like Op. 10/3–I, m. 93–105, is in double counterpoint; but the part in eighth-notes has an embellishing rather than a thematic significance); Op. 31/1–III, m. 17 ff.

Countermelodic phrases or fragments are often used to embellish a repetition (Op. 10/3–II: compare m. 17–19 with 21–23) or as bridge-like fillers (Op. 13–II, m. 37 ff.) between phrases of the principal voice.

Many illustrations of semi-contrapuntal treatment can be found in Exs. 54, 55 and 56. Special attention should be paid to those cases where the harmony becomes richer through the movement of the voices; and where the motive of the accompaniment involves a characteristic rhythmic figure, often the result of a more or less free imitation.

Both semi- and quasi-counterpoint are illustrated in Op. 10/1–I. In m. 48–55 both upper voices are so well organized that it is difficult to say which is main voice and which is countermelody. In the continuation (m. 56–85), the bass moves more melodically than the presentation of the harmony would require, without, however, becoming a countermelody.

The lowest voice in Op. 14/2–I, m. 49 ff., imitates quasi-contrapuntally only the phrasing of the melody. Similarly, the auxiliaries in Op. 31/1–II, m. 16 ff., though disguised as imitations, embellish sustained tones of the harmony. The imitations of Op. 28–IV, m. 28–31 and 33–35, are definitely not contrapuntal, since they present only one harmony.

TREATMENT OF THE BASS LINE

Except in the case of a pedal point, the bass should participate in every change of the harmony. One must not forget that the bass should be treated like a secondary melody, which means that it should remain (except for special purposes) within a single register and possess a certain degree of continuity (Exs. 44g, i, j, k, 45i, 46u, 51b). The ear is trained to pay much attention to the bass. Even a short note is understood as a continuing bass until another bass note can be heard as a (melodic) continuation.

For the sake of fluency a bass which is not countermelodic should make free use of inversions, even where they are not harmonically necessary (Exs. 45g, 46c, g, 51f, 58d, 59g).

TREATMENT OF THE MOTIVE OF THE ACCOMPANIMENT

In many cases a single motive of accompaniment is used consistently throughout a whole section, except for cadences. This is possible only in the most primitive cases, in which the harmony does not change much, and the motive is readily adaptable (e.g. the obsolete Alberti bass).

Changes of character or construction, or increase in the number of harmonies, may justify or even require modification of the accompaniment. A clear change in all these respects is found in Op. 14/2–I; compare m. 1–4 with m. 5 ff. In Op. 31/1–II, where the climactic ascension in the melody requires richer harmony, the motive of accompaniment is modified accordingly (m. 5). In Op. 31/3–III, the special form of the broken chord figure is reduced (m. 3 ff.) to no more than is necessary to keep up the motus.

The motive of the accompaniment, as a unifying device, should be maintained for at least several measures or phrases. Even if varied, it should not disappear completely. But cases exist in which more than one figure is used, especially in Mozart's Rococo style, as many of the excerpts in Exs. 45 and 59 prove.

Harmonic requirements in the vicinity of cadences or half cadences often force modification or liquidation of the motive of accompaniment. This process may take a variety of forms. See, for instance, Exs. 45*f*, 46*j*, 48*c*, 51*a*, 55*a*, *b*, 56*b*, 58*e*, 59*g*, *h*, 61*d*.

REQUIREMENTS OF INSTRUMENTS

In piano writing the necessity of keeping the accompaniment within reach of the fingers sometimes requires co-operation of both hands (Op. 2/3–I, m. 141 ff.; Op. 13–II, m. 41–42 ff.) or a shift from hand to hand—with or without a change of register (Op. 27/2–I, m. 15–16, 23–24; Op. 31/2–I, m. 28 ff.). Changes of register also take place for reasons of expressiveness or sonority.

In writing for other than keyboard instruments, the individual parts should be elaborated more independently, in order to sustain the interest of the players. But there is danger of imbalance produced by too rich an accompaniment. Economy and transparency are indispensable.

The variety of chamber-music combinations precludes detailed discussion of the accompaniment. But, intelligently applied, the principles are the same as for keyboard instruments.

Ex. 62

a) *Wagner,* Tannhäuser Overture

etc.

b) *Beethoven,* Piano Trio, Op. 97 - III

Andante cantabile

c) *Schubert,* Die Nebensonnen

d) *Beethoven,* String Quartet, Op. 132 - III

Molto adagio

Ex. 63
a) Op.7-III, Minore

Ex. 64
a) *Chopin*, Fantaisie-Impromptu, Op.66
Allegro agitato

b) *Chopin*, Etude, Op.10/10

c) *Chopin*, Ballade No.4, Op.52

d) *von Bülow's* transcription, Wagner's "Tristan"

e) *Schubert,* Op.25, Das Wandern

Das Wan-dern ist des Mül-lers Lust, das Wan - dern

f) *Brahms,* Horn Trio, Op.40, Finale
Allegro con brio

Ex. 65

Ex. 66
a) *Brahms*, Handel Variations, Op. 24-Var. 3

b) *Beethoven*, Trio, Op. 97-III

Piano *p*

Cello

c) *Beethoven*, String Quartet, Op. 127-I

m. 89

etc.

Ex. 67
a) *Beethoven*, String Quartet, Op. 59/2-III

Rhythmic
excerpt

Motus

Dominant region of relative major

VII

etc.

Variant for cadence

b) *Beethoven*, String Quartet, Op. 59/1-IV

m. 73

c) *Beethoven*, String Quartet, Op. 59/3-1

m. 149

X

CHARACTER AND MOOD

THE concept that music expresses something is generally accepted.

However, chess does not tell stories. Mathematics does not evoke emotions. Similarly, from the viewpoint of pure aesthetics, music does not express the extramusical.

But from the viewpoint of psychology, our capacity for mental and emotional associations is as unlimited as our capacity for repudiating them is limited. Thus every ordinary object can provoke musical associations, and, conversely, music can evoke associations with extramusical objects.

Many composers have composed under the urge to express emotional associations. Moreover, programme music goes so far as to narrate entire stories with musical symbols. There also exist a great variety of 'characteristic pieces' expressing every conceivable mood.

There are *Nocturnes, Ballades, Funeral Marches, Romances, Scenes from Childhood, Flower Pieces, Novelettes,* etc., by Chopin and Schumann. There are Beethoven's *Eroica* and *Pastorale* Symphonies; Berlioz's *Roman Carnival*; Tchaikovsky's *Romeo and Juliet*; Strauss's *Thus Spake Zarathustra*; Debussy's *La Mer*; Sibelius's *Swan of Tuonela*; and a multitude of others. Finally, there are songs, choir music, oratorios, operas, melodramas, ballets and motion-picture music.

All these categories are intended to produce not only musical impressions, but also to provoke secondary effects: associations of a definite character.

The term *character*, applied to music, refers not only to the emotion which the piece should produce and the mood in which it was composed, but also the manner in which it must be played. It is fallacious to think that the tempo indications determine character. In classical music, at least, this is not true. There is not one adagio character, but hundreds; not one scherzo character, but thousands. An adagio is slow; an allegro is fast. This contributes something, but not everything, to the expression of a character.

The type of accompaniment plays an important role in the establishment of character. No player could express the character of a march if the accompaniment were that of a chorale; no one could play a restful adagio melody if the accompaniment were like a torrent.

Old dance forms were characterized by certain rhythms in the accompaniment, which were also reflected in the melody. These rhythmic characteristics are the principal means of distinguishing a mazurka, for example, from a gavotte or a polka. But, in general, rhythmic features help to establish the mood and special character of an individual piece, as well as to provide the structurally necessary internal contrasts.

The concept of difference in character can be clarified by comparison of three movements from Beethoven sonatas which are similar in that they express something 'stormy' or 'passionate' (Op. 27/2–III; Op. 31/2–I; Op. 57–I). The differences in character manifest themselves not only in the thematic material of the openings, but also in the nature of the continuations. Compare the respective subordinate themes: Op. 27/2–III, m. 21 ff.; Op. 31/2–I, m. 41 ff.; Op. 57–I, m. 35 ff.

How little the tempo alone contributes to character will be realized if one compares these three with three others in rapid tempo: the Presto Agitato of Op. 27/2–III with the Allegro Vivace of Op. 31/1–I; or the Allegro of Op. 31/2–I with the Allegro of Op. 31/3–I; or the Assai Allegro of Op. 57–I with the Presto alla Tedesca of Op. 79–I.

But the changes of character within a single movement—even within its smaller sections—are even more important. Apart from the strong contrast between principal and subordinate themes in Op. 57–I, there are many other contrasts. Note the sudden change of texture in m. 24, its intensification in m. 28 ff., and its gradual liquidation, m. 31 ff. How dramatic is the change of expression when 'dolce legato', m. 35, replaces the previous hard staccato of the left hand; and when the movement suddenly stops in m. 41. A new and even stronger contrast in texture (m. 51) changes the entire aspect of the rest of this section.

This is not a singular case. All good music consists of many contrasting ideas. An idea achieves distinctness and validity in contrast with others. Heraclitus called contrast 'the principle of development'. Musical thinking is subject to the same dialectic as all other thinking.

Differences of character may have an influence on the structure, but no particular character can be said to demand a particular form. Though one would scarcely write a waltz in the form of a symphony, Beethoven wrote the first movement of a sonata (Op. 54) 'In tempo d'un Menuetto'; and his Seventh Symphony, because of its character, is commonly called the 'Dance Symphony'. But, in general, light, graceful, simple moods will not require complicated forms nor adventurous elaboration. On the other hand, profound ideas, deeply moving emotions, heroic attitudes, require the bold contrasts and thorough elaboration of more complex forms.

Descriptive music—such as programme music; stage, ballet and moving picture music; melodramas; and even songs—under pressure of strong and sudden contrasts, develops its forms in harmony with those emotions, events and actions which it is supposed to illustrate. In such cases the basic motive itself possesses a descriptive character or mood as illustrated in Ex. 68.

In the second movement of Beethoven's *Pastorale* Symphony (Ex. 68a), the sound of the murmuring brook is illustrated by the flowing movement of the accompaniment. Ex. 68b, the Magic Fire Music from Wagner's *Die Walküre*, expresses musically the flickering flames. With an equally rich movement, Smetana describes the source of the River Moldau (Ex. 68c). Bach's *St. Matthew Passion* is rich in illustrative passages. Among them, particularly striking because it appears in a recitative, is the description of the rending of the curtain (Ex. 68d). The swing of the weathervane is depicted in Schubert's *The Weathervane*, and characteristically enough, the trills in m. 4 and 5 represent its creaking (Ex. 68e).

In composing even the smallest exercises, the student should never fail to keep in mind a special character. A poem, a story, a play or a moving picture may provide the stimulus to express definite moods. The pieces which he composes should differ widely. Especially fruitful are differences in tempo, rhythm and metre. Such practice will help him to acquire the capacity to produce the manifold types of contrast necessary for larger forms.

Ex. 68

a) *Beethoven,* Symphony No. 6 "By the brook"

b) *Wagner,* Die Walküre, Act III, "Magic Fire Music"

c) *Smetana,* "Vltava"

m.17-18

d) *Bach,* St. Matthew Passion

Evangelist

Und sie - he da, der Vor - hang im Tem - pel zer -

Basso Continuo

riss in zwei Stück, von o - ben an bis un - ten

aus. Und die Er - de er - be - be - te

e) *Schubert,* "Die Wetterfähne"

XI

MELODY AND THEME

THE concentration of the main idea in a single melodic line requires a special kind of balance and organization, only partly explicable in terms of technique. Instinctively, every music lover knows what a melody is. Instinctively, also, one who has talent may be able to write a melody without technical advice. But such melodies seldom possess the perfection of higher art. Therefore some guidance, based on musical literature, as well as on historical, aesthetic and technical considerations, will be provided.

Instrumental melodies admit much more freedom in every respect than vocal. But freedom prospers best when under control. Accordingly, the restrictions of vocal melody offer a sounder starting-point.

VOCAL MELODY

A melody could hardly include unmelodious elements; the concept of the melodious is intimately related to the concept of singableness. The nature and technique of the primordial musical instrument, the voice, determines what is singable. The concept of the melodious in instrumental melody has developed as a free adaptation from the vocal model.

Singableness, in a more popular sense, implies relatively long notes; smooth linkage of the registers; movement in waves, more stepwise than by leaps; avoidance of augmented and diminished intervals; adherence to the tonality and its most closely related regions; employment of the natural intervals of a key; gradual modulation; and a cautious use of dissonance.

Additional restrictions derive from the registers of the voice, and from the difficulties of intonation (unless he possesses a memory for absolute pitch, the singer has no yardstick whatever for intonation).

The highest register of a voice is 'vulnerable'; its use is always a strain on the singer. To remain too long in it tires the voice. But used carefully, it really produces a climax, for which it should be reserved (a structural consideration). The lowest register is stronger than the middle register, but should not be overburdened with too much dramatic expression. The middle register is not capable of extreme expression and offers no great dynamic compass, but within these limits it is the most convenient register of every voice. And the registers differ not only in volume, but also in colour (timbre). Sudden changes of register endanger the unity of tone quality, a difficulty which, however, well-trained artists know how to overcome. The voice needs a certain minimal time to develop a full sound. Accordingly, rapid notes, especially staccatos, and such notes as ask for a strong accentuation (sforzati, etc.), are difficult, though they are not beyond the ability of a virtuoso.

Support of intonation, through harmony, is almost indispensable, especially at the beginning. Chromaticism, augmented intervals (or successions of them), and tones (or tone successions) which cannot be related to the harmony, especially if outside the tonality, offer difficulties.

Of course, not all the augmented or diminished intervals in Ex. 69, when accompanied by comprehensible harmony, are excessively difficult. But some, like *e, f, m, n, o, p, q, r* and *t* are not easy. Successive leaps like those in Ex. 70, having a compass of a seventh or ninth, should be avoided.

Chromaticism is difficult partly because the natural semi-tones differ in size from the tempered (a fact which causes choirs to get off pitch[1]); but sparingly used it need not be avoided. The dissonances in Exs. 71*a–d*, as circumscribing or embellishing notes, can easily be understood. Such cases as those in Exs. 71*e–g* require highly developed technical skill, while those of Ex. 72 are difficult to justify.

Prior to the great changes which began in the first quarter of the nineteenth century, aestheticians could define melody in terms of beauty, expressiveness, simplicity, naturalness, tunefulness, singableness, unity, proportion and balance. But taking into account the development of harmony and its influence on every concept of musical aesthetics, it is obvious that earlier definitions of 'theme' and 'melody', 'melodious' and 'unmelodious', are no longer adequate.

Illustrations from the literature

Each of the quotations from the vocal literature (Exs. 73–91) contradicts in some respect the older limitations imposed on melody.

Among the examples from Schubert's *Winterreise*, Op. 89, the modulation in the fifth measure of Ex. 73*a* is unusually sudden and remote. In Ex. 73*b* a leap of a tenth appears; and in Ex. 73*c* the 'Stormy Morning' is pictured so realistically and in such rapid tempo that it becomes difficult to sing.

In Ex. 74*a* (Brahms) the range spans an eleventh within two measures; in Ex. 74*b* a syncopated rhythm almost obscures the phrasing; in Ex. 74*c*, 'The Forge', the illustration of the upswinging hammer precludes a natural legato and forces upon the voice a staccato accentuation. But in Ex. 74*d* Brahms contradicts his own rule: 'The melody of a song should be such that one could whistle it' (i.e. without accompaniment, without the support of an explanatory harmony). Try to whistle this melody!

Difficulties of intonation are also involved in Ex. 75 (Grieg), Ex. 76 (Wolf) and Ex. 77 (Mahler). In the latter example not only the intervals and the rapid tempo,

---

[1] A singer should be trained to the intervals of the tempered scale, which is a convention deviating from the natural acoustical intervals, to assure correct musical intonation.

but especially the passionate expression, makes the impression of an instrumental, rather than a vocal, melody.

Such treatment of the voice is largely attributable to Richard Wagner who, for dramatic purposes, often went beyond the limits of the voice. Observe, in the wonderful melody of Ex. 78a, how often he uses the highest register in this explosive outburst of emotion; how suddenly he jumps to the lowest register; what difficult and dissonant intervals are included within short phrases; how many syllables have to be pronounced in this rapid tempo (x); and observe especially the ending of this section (xx) with a leap of a ninth. Exs. 78b, c and d are historically interesting, since Wagner's great critical opponent, Eduard Hanslick, maliciously quoted them to ridicule Wagner's 'melodious' voice writing.

No wonder that Debussy (Ex. 79) and Richard Strauss (Ex. 80), as followers of most of Wagner's musico-dramatic principles, took advantage of this progress in writing for the voice, progress in writing which did not turn out to enhance singability.

The Italian composers, renowned for their great understanding and respect for the voice, could not escape Wagner's influence. The Italian singer's facility in rapid enunciation (even superior to that of the French and Spanish), and in pronouncing many successive syllables, has always allowed Italian composers to write such rapid small notes as in Ex. 81, from Rossini's *Barber of Seville*. By comparison, the examples from German music, Mozart's *Magic Flute* (Ex. 82), Beethoven's *Fidelio* (Ex. 83) and Schubert's *Ungeduld* (Ex. 84), seem slow; and so does the French example from Auber's *Fra Diavolo* (Ex. 85). But Verdi, in *Otello* (Ex. 86), surpasses these latter in velocity, and surpasses Rossini in difficulty, by using a chromatic scale (x), and by introducing a surprising change of metre (xx).

Melodic progressions, like those of Moussorgsky (Ex. 87), undoubtedly influenced by Oriental folk-music, in turn influenced Western melodic writing. The example from Puccini (Ex. 88) is also folkloristic (pseudo-Chinese). Though Puccini was always progressive in his harmony, the extreme modernism of this example is exceptional.

On the other hand, in Ex. 89, the music of Tchaikovsky, a contemporary of Moussorgsky, shows no relation to folklore, but rather to the average harmonic feeling of the epoch; it resembles music of the Norwegian, Grieg (Ex. 75), more than that of his Russian compatriots.

The examples from Bizet's *Carmen* (Ex. 90) and from songs by Schoenberg (Ex. 91) are based on extended tonality. The ear of the modern musician has gradually acquired the capacity to comprehend the most remote harmonies as coherent elements of a tonality. To composers of the Wagnerian and post-Wagnerian epoch, the use of such intervals and progressions as in Ex. 91, even in melodies, was as natural as the use of scalewise movement or broken chords to their predecessors.

The preceding discussion has perhaps only clarified the limits of the melodious, but has not determined what is unmelodious.

Imbalance, incoherence, inadequate integration with the harmony or accompaniment, incongruity of phrasing and rhythm, are criteria of the unmelodious. A musician of the nineties might have objected to Ex. 80*b* from Strauss's *Salome*, on the grounds that the multitude of incoherent rhythmic features produces imbalance, and makes the phrasing—which should contribute to understanding—incomprehensible. Moreover, it would be difficult to imagine with what harmony the melody of Ex. 80*a* could be integrated.

But in works of the post-Wagnerian composers, the voice does not always have the main melody (an excuse—but only an excuse—for imbalance). Where so many features contradict the melodious, the man of the nineties would not be entirely wrong to call these cases unmelodious. However, with the passage of time the concepts have changed considerably.

INSTRUMENTAL MELODY

The freedom of instrumental melodies is also restricted by the technical limitations of the various instruments. These limitations differ in nature and degree, particularly with respect to the compass, from those of vocal music. Nevertheless, an instrumental melody should still be such that, ideally, it could be sung, if only by a voice of incredible capacity.

To the contemporary ear the difference between instrumental and vocal melodies in classical music does not seem very great. With slight changes the difference can be eliminated. For instance, the leading subject of Beethoven's Rondo, Op. 2/2-IV, is distinctly pianistic. In Ex. 92 the brilliant arpeggio of the first measure is simplified, which automatically eliminates the large leap of m. 2. The result is a perfectly singable melody. Such adaptation to the requirements of the voice was often used in classical operas. Sometimes, when the voice repeated an instrumental melody from the prelude, the melody was simplified, as in Ex. 93; or embellished as in Ex. 94.

But even in the Beethoven piano sonatas there are many melodies which could be sung by any singer. See, for example, the leading subjects of Op. 2/2-II; Op. 7-IV; Op. 10/1-II; Op. 10/3-III; Op. 13-II, etc.

Many sections, in instrumental music, cannot be called melodies, though they may contain nothing unmelodious. Some are étude-like, e.g. Op. 7-IV, m. 64; Op. 10/2-I, m. 95 ff.; Op. 22-IV, the semi-contrapuntal section, m. 72–79. But others must be classified as themes,[1] which, precisely defined, differ markedly from melodies in structure and tendency.

MELODY VERSUS THEME

The term *theme* is here used to characterize specific types of structures, of which many examples can be found in sonatas, symphonies, etc. Perhaps the most clearcut

---

[1] This term is one of the most misused terms in the musical vocabulary. It is applied without discrimination to many different structures.

among the Beethoven piano sonatas are the leading subjects of Op. 53–I, Op. 57–I,
Op. 27/2–III and Op. 111–I.

The clarification of both concepts will best be accomplished by a comparison of
melody and theme.

Every succession of tones produces unrest, conflict, problems. One single tone is
not problematic because the ear defines it as a tonic, a point of repose. Every added
tone makes this determination questionable. Every musical form can be considered
as an attempt to treat this unrest either by halting or limiting it, or by solving the
problem. A melody re-establishes repose through balance. A theme solves the problem by carrying out its consequences. The unrest in a melody need not reach below
the surface, while the problem of a theme may penetrate to the profoundest depths.

Since rhythmic characteristics are less decisive in a melody, it could be called two-
dimensional, comprising chiefly interval and latent harmony. On the other hand, the
importance of rhythmic development makes the problem of the theme three-dimen-
sional. (See, for example, Beethoven, Op. 10/1–I, Op. 27/2–III, Op. 14/2–I, Exs.
95a, b.)

Thus a melody can be compared to an 'aperçu', an 'aphorism', in its rapid advance
from problem to solution. But a theme resembles rather a scientific hypothesis which
does not convince without a number of tests, without presentation of proof.

The melody also tends to achieve balance in the most direct way. It avoids intensify-
ing the unrest; it supports comprehensibility by limitation, and facilitates lucidity
through subdivision; it extends itself rather by continuation than by elaboration or
development. It uses slightly varied motive-forms, which achieve variety by presenting
the basic features in different situations. It remains within the closer harmonic
relationships.

All these restrictions and limitations produce that *independence* and *self-determina-
tion* because of which a melody requires no addition, continuation or elaboration.

In contrast, a state of repose will scarcely be reached or attempted early in a theme;
it will generally sharpen its problem (bringing it to a point) or deepen it. (Beethoven,
Op. 53–I, Op. 57–I, Op. 31/1–I, Op. 31/2–I.)

Subdivision, often similar to that of a melody, may occur in a theme (Op. 90–I,
Op. 2/2–I). In a melody the separation is seldom definite, so as to offer an opening for,
or a bridge to, a continuation. In themes remotely coherent segments are often
juxtaposed in a co-ordinate meaning, without connectives (Op. 90–I, Op. 14/2–I).
Seldom is a theme extended by spinning a continuation for mere formal balance;
rather, it leaps directly to remote developments of the basic motive (Op. 10/1–I, m.
9, 17; Op. 7–I; Op. 31/2–I; Ex. 95c).

The formulation of a theme assumes that there will follow 'adventures', 'predica-
ments', which ask for solution, for elaboration, for development, for contrast (the
implications are discussed more fully in Chapter XX). The harmony of a theme is often

active, 'roving', unstable. Nevertheless, and in spite of remote harmonies, one will find that even complex themes still move around a tonic, or a definite contrasting region (Brahms, First Symphony–I; Piano Quartet, Op. 60–I; Beethoven, Op. 53–I). The organization cannot be so loose that one might feel a lack of structure.

A *theme* is not at all independent and self-determined. On the contrary, it is strictly bound to consequences which have to be drawn, and without which it may appear insignificant.

A *melody*, classic or contemporary, tends toward regularity, simple repetitions and even symmetry. Hence, it generally reveals distinct phrasing. Of course, the length of a singer's breath is no measure for the length of a phrase in an instrumental melody, but the number of measures in moderate tempo is likely to be about the same as in a vocal melody.

Theory must be stricter than reality. It is forced to generalize, and that means reduction on the one hand, exaggeration on the other. This description necessarily exaggerates the difference between melody and theme. Hybrid forms exist. Sometimes a melody elaborates its rhythmical problems, or implies remote harmonies, or is structurally complicated, or draws consequences, or is followed by development. On the other hand, many a theme contains melodic segments, or is based on the simple construction of the period, or is treated as if it were independent.

All the previous statements are of limited or relative validity. Time has not only produced a development of the technical means, and widened the concept of theme and melody in creative minds; it has also changed our comprehension of music written in preceding epochs. In consequence of this development, nobody today would hesitate to consider the two themes from Beethoven's string quartets in Exs. 96a and b as melodies, although they are structurally instrumental themes. This impression is perhaps supported by the phrasing, which is that of a melody. But Ex. 96c could never have failed to make the impression of a melody, although there is only a single symptom—singableness. All the other symptoms are missing—no section or phrase is repeated; there is no distinct motive or motive-form; and the segments, m. 17–22, 25–27 and 29–30 develop a figure (which previously appeared in the viola, m. 13) in a manner which is usual in a theme rather than a melody.

Exs. 97, 98, 99 and 100 show the tonal contour of a number of melodies. It was mentioned previously that melodies proceed in waves, a fact which can readily be observed here. The amplitude of these waves varies. A melody seldom moves long in one direction. Though the student was advised to avoid repeating the culmination point, the climax, the graphs show that many a good melody does so. The student had better not attempt it.

In the music of our predecessors, somewhat modified instrumental melodies (especially in operas and oratorios) were often used also for the singers. In those days the difference between vocal and instrumental melodies was not very great. It is greater today, partly because the ability of the singers has not developed as much as the technique of instrumentalists. Worse, the mental capacity of singers to deal with a more modern kind of melodic line is utterly inadequate to the requirements. Perhaps at no time has the gap between creation and performance been more discouraging, the difference between those who call themselves 'artists' and those others who have proved to be creators.

The melody is certainly a simpler formulation than the theme. Condensation does not admit a too detailed elaboration; concentration of the content in a single line excludes presentation of remote consequences. Nevertheless, this formulation permits much more than the expression of popular ideas and commonplace feelings in a superficial manner. Aesthetically, as well as for sound reasons of economy, there is no nobler contrast than to speak lightly of a great grief.

> *Aus meinen grossen Schmerzen*
> *Mach ich die kleinen Lieder. . . .*
> (Heine, *Buch der Lieder*)

So heroes belittle their wounds and their achievements—this is the modesty of great men.

Ex.72

Ex.73
a) *Schubert,* "Auf dem Flusse"

b) "Irrlicht"

c) "Der Stürmische Morgen"

Ex.74
a) *Brahms,* "Der Gang zum Liebchen"

b) "Minnelied"

c) "Der Schmitt" (The Forge)
  (*accents not in the original*)

My   true   love   I   hear,   his   ham - mer   up - swing-ing

d) "Treue Liebe"

Ex.75
Grieg, "Autumn Thoughts"

Ex.76
a) *Hugo Wolf*, "Peregrina" I
m. 6-8

b) m.15-16

Ex.77
a) *Mahler*, "Das Lied von der Erde"

b) "Lied des Verfolgten im Thurme"

Ex.78
a) *Wagner*, Die Meistersinger, Act III

Eva:
O Sachs! mein Freund! Du theu - rer Mann   Wie ich dur Ed - lem

loh - nen kann   Was oh - ne dei - ne Lie - be___ was wär' ich oh - ne

dich   ob je auch Kind ich blie - be   er - weck - test du mich nicht?

and finally
du wär-est mein Ge-mahl,   den Preis - - reicht' ich___ nur dir

b) Act I, *Magdalene:*
Komm, Kind!   Nun hast du Spang und Tuch   c)   mit Ev' - chens Schut-ze

d)

Was Küch und Kel-ler,

Ex.79

Debussy, Pelléas et Mélisande

Je vais fuir en cri-ant de joie et de dou-leur comme un a-veu-gle etc.

Ex.80

a) *Richard Strauss*, Salome

Herodes

Du wirst schön sein als Kö - ni-gin un-er-mess-lich schön

b)

Salome

Ich will mit mein-en Zäh - nen   hin-ein-beis-sen   wie man in ein-e rei-

- fe Frucht beis - sen mag

Ex.81

Rossini, The Barber of Seville

Lar - go al fac-to-tum del-la cit-tà   etc. and   La-la- la-la-la-la-la-la-la etc.

Ex.82

Mozart, The Magic Flute

Allegro

Al - les fühlt der Lie-be Freu-den schnä-belt tän-delt, herzt und küsst.

Ex.83

Beethoven, Fidelio

Allegro vivace

O, na - men; na - men-lo - se Freu-de!

Ex.84

Schubert, Ungeduld

Poco vivace

Ich schatt' es gern in al - le Rin-den ein, ich grüb' es gern in je-den Kie-sel-stein

Ex. 85
Auber, Fra Diavolo

Ex. 86
a) *Verdi,* Otello

I - naf - fia lu - go___ la!_____ trin-ca, tra - can - na

b)

Be - va, be - va,   be - - - - - - va

Ex. 87
Moussorgsky, Khovantstchina

Ex. 88
Puccini, Turandot, Act 2, Scene 1

etc.

Ex.89
Tschaikowsky, Eugen Onegin

Ex.90
Bizet, Carmen, Act 1

Ex.91
a) *Schoenberg,* Op.6/1, "Traumleben"

Aus mein - en   Nak - ken schliesst sich ein   blü - then-wei - sser   Arm

Es ruht____ auf mei-nem Mun - de ein Früh-ling jung und warm.

b) *Schoenberg,* Op.10, String Quartet No.2-IV

Ich   lö - se   mich in   Tö - nen,   kreisend____   etc.

Ex. 92
Op. 2/2 - IV

Ex. 93
Mozart, The Magic Flute
Flute

Tenor

Wie stark ist nicht dein Zau - ber - ton, Weil, hol - - - - de___

etc.

Flö - te, hol - de Flö - te___ durch___ dein Spie - - len

Ex. 94
Rossini, The Barber of Seville, Act I
Largo, (Instrumental Prelude)

tr

Voice

tr

10

Ex. 95

a) *Brahms*, Trio, Op. 87-I

b) Trio, Op. 101-I

c) Piano Quintet, Op 34-I

Allegro non troppo

Piano

Ex. 96

a) *Beethoven*, String Quartet, Op. 132-III

b) String Quartet, Op. 132-I

Allegro Va.

m. 23   Vlc.

c) String Quartet, Op. 95-II

Allegretto ma non troppo

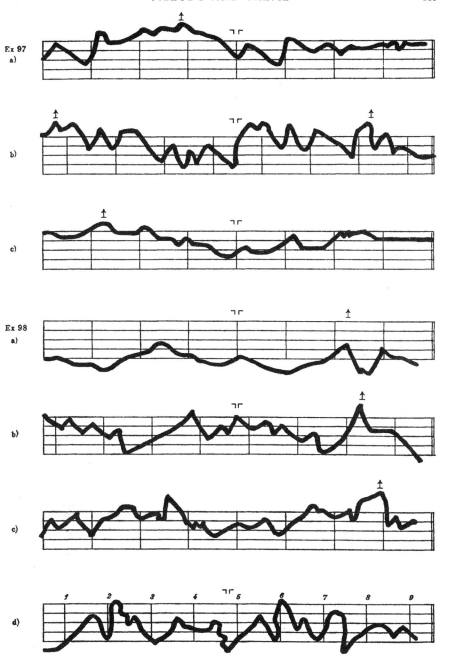

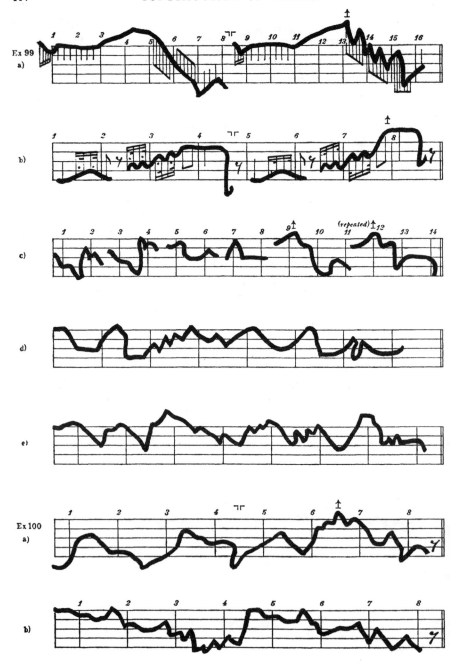

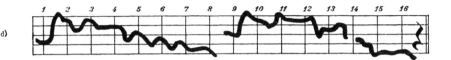

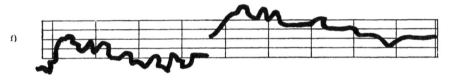

Ex. 97 Contours from *English Suites* by J.S. Bach

a) Sarabande, Suite No.1 (A) ¾
m. 1-8, period

b) Gavotte No.1, Suite No.3 (g minor) ²⁄₂
m. 1-8, period

c) Sarabande, Suite No. 6 (d minor) ³⁄₂
m. 1-8, period

Ex. 98 Contours from *String Quartets* by Haydn

a) Adagio (C) ²⁄₄, Op. 76/1-II
m. 1-8, period

b) Finale (B♭) ²⁄₂, Op. 76/4-IV
m. 1-8, period

c) Allegretto (D) ⁶⁄₈, Op. 76/5-I
m. 1-8, period

d) Largo (F♯) ₵, Op. 76/5-II
m. 1-9, irregular period

Ex. 99 Contours from Compositions by Mozart

a) Menuetto (D) ¾, String Quartet K.V. 575-III
m. 1-16, period

b) Andante (A♭) ²⁄₄, from Symphony K.V. 543-II
m. 1-8, period

c) Cherubino's Aria ("Non sa più cosa son")
from *The Marriage of Figaro*
Allegro vivace (E♭) ₵
m. 2-15

d) Allegretto grazioso (B♭) ₵, Piano Sonata K.V. 333-I
m. 1-8, period

e) Allegro (B♭) ₵, Piano Sonata K.V. 281-III
m. 1-8, period

Ex. 100 Contours from *Piano Sonatas* by Beethoven

a) Adagio (F) ¾, Op. 2/1-II
m. 1-8, period

b) Poco allegretto e grazioso (E♭) ²⁄₄, Op. 7-IV
m. 1-8, period

c) Finale: Prestissimo (c minor) ₵, Op. 10/1-III
m. 1-8, period

d) Menuetto (D) ¾, Op. 10/3-III
m. 1-16, period

e) Adagio (E♭) ⁹⁄₈, Op. 22-II
m. 2-9

f) Assai Allegro (f minor) ¹²⁄₈, Op. 57-I
m. 36-44

XII

ADVICE FOR SELF-CRITICISM

THE preceding discussion of melody and theme is chiefly aesthetic, rather than technical. Technical advice can be formulated more easily in the negative than in the positive. The sense of melody enables one who has it to do the right thing at once without the intervention of self-criticism, but even a master may stray on to the wrong track. When such a deviation occurs, one has to discover where and why one erred, and which is the right track. And therefore, self-criticism is necessary to a composer, gifted or not.

The best tool of a musician is his ear. Therefore:

1. LISTEN[1]

Play or read harmony and melody separately several times. This sometimes prevents self-deception. Perhaps only one of these factors is poor, its shortcomings hidden behind the virtues of the other. If the harmonic progression is satisfactory the beginner may easily overlook shortcomings in his melody. A good melody should be smooth, fluent and balanced when it is played without accompaniment.

2. ANALYSE

Be conscious of the significant features of the basic motive, and determine whether they, or the less characteristic, are developed. There may be empty segments with no real content, without significant melodic or rhythmic movement, even without harmonic change.

3. ELIMINATE NON-ESSENTIALS

Too much variation, too much embellishment and figuration, excessively remote motive-variations, too abrupt a change of register, may contribute to imbalance.

4. AVOID MONOTONY

Too many repetitions of tones or melodic figures are annoying, if they do not exploit the advantage of a repetition—emphasis. Watch especially the highest tone of the melody. The climax normally appears toward the end, and can be repeated or

[1] Every good musician must possess the 'inner ear', auditory imagery, the capacity of hearing music in imagination.

exceeded only with caution. Beware of too restricted a compass, and avoid moving too long in one direction. Evaluate sensitively the endings of the phrases.

5. WATCH THE BASS LINE

The bass was previously described as a 'second melody'. This means that it is subject to somewhat the same requirements as the principal melody. It should be rhythmically balanced, should avoid the monotony of unnecessary repetitions, should have some variety of contour, and should make full use of inversions (especially of seventh chords). Chromatic progression can be as melodically advantageous in the bass as in the principal melody. Semi- and quasi-counterpoint, such as can be seen in Exs. 44g, i, j, 48a and 58g, help to make the bass interesting.

ILLUSTRATIONS OF SELF-CRITICISM

Ex. 105,[1] a small ternary form with a number of alternative contrasting middle sections, can be used to show the application of some of these precepts.

In Ex. 105a the break in continuity at the end of the second phrase (m. 4) seems too pronounced. The discontinuity is intensified by the stepwise progression across the bar line. The addition of a connective chord (small notes) maintains the melodic and rhythmic flow and enhances the harmonic logic. Similarly, the half-note in the first half of m. 8 is somewhat weak and empty. The small notes keep the melody alive to the end of the phrase.

More generally, one might point out that the repeated notes in the first eight measures are somewhat overdone, as are the parallel thirds in the last half. Of course, these features are intended to demonstrate in easily recognizable form the use of motival characteristics.

In Ex. 105c the chromatic return to V at the last moment is too crowded with rapid harmonic change to balance the preceding sparse harmonization. Moreover, it would not connect well with m. 13 of Ex. 105a.

The active movement in Ex. 105f is hardly adequate to disguise the rather static harmony.

Ex. 105g, on the other hand, is so filled with remote and rapidly changing harmonies that it fails to balance the preceding and following sections of Ex. 105a.

6. MAKE MANY SKETCHES

Change the method of variation frequently. Try each method several times. Join the best sketches to produce others and improve them until the result is satisfactory.

To make sketches is a humble and unpretentious approach toward perfection. A beginner who is not too self-assured, who does not believe too firmly in his

[1] Exs. 101–7 after Chapter XIII, p. 126.

'infallibility', and who knows that he has not yet reached technical maturity, will consider everything he writes as tentative. Later he will be able to base his composing exclusively on his sense of form.

The student should frequently review the methods of motive variation. Methodical variation is no substitute for invention, but it may be stimulating, like the athlete's 'warm-up'.

7. WATCH THE HARMONY; WATCH THE ROOT PROGRESSIONS; WATCH THE BASS LINE

PART II

SMALL FORMS

XIII

THE SMALL TERNARY FORM

(A–B–A¹)

AN overwhelming proportion of musical forms is structurally composed of three parts. The third part is sometimes a true repetition (recapitulation) of the first, but oftener it is a more or less modified repetition. The second part is organized as a contrast.

This form may derive from the early 'Rondeau', in which interludes were inserted between repetitions of a refrain. Repetition satisfies the desire to hear again what was pleasing at first hearing, and simultaneously aids comprehension. A contrast, however, is useful to avoid the possibility of monotony.

Sections producing contrasts of various types and degrees are to be found in a great many forms: e.g. Small Ternary Form (formerly called Three-Part Song Form); larger ternary forms, such as Minuet or Scherzo; and Sonata or Symphony.

Contrast presupposes coherence. Incoherent contrast, though tolerated in 'descriptive' music, is intolerable in a well organized form. Contrasting sections, therefore, must utilize the same processes by which motive-forms are connected in simpler formulations.

THE SMALL TERNARY FORM

The A-section of the A–B–A¹ form may be a sentence or a period, ending on I, V or III (iii) in major; on i, III, V, or v in minor. The beginning, at least, should clearly express the tonality, because of the contrast to follow.

The A¹-section, the recapitulation, ends on the tonic if it completes an independent piece. It is seldom an unchanged repetition. The final cadence generally differs from that of the first section, even if both lead to the same degree.

THE CONTRASTING MIDDLE SECTION

The most effective factor in a contrasting section is the harmony. The A-section establishes a tonic; the B-section contraposes another region (one of the more closely related). This provides both contrast and coherence.

Further coherence is furnished by the metre, and by using forms of the basic motive which are not too remote from those of the A-section.

Further contrast can be achieved through the use of new variations of the basic motive, or change in the order of previous motive-forms.

Illustrations from the literature: Beethoven, piano sonatas

The opening of the Adagio of Beethoven's Op. 2/1, m. 1–16, reveals a structure from which a practice form can be abstracted. Its A-section, a period with a caesura on V in m. 4, comprises eight measures. The A¹-section is condensed to four measures (m. 13–16). The B-section is the simplest possible model of an effective contrast. It comprises four measures, built from a two-measure phrase and a varied repetition of it. This construction, two units, the second a more or less varied repetition of the first, possesses an obvious natural logic. The mere interchange of V and I in the B-section is a coherent contrast to the interchange of I and V at the beginning. The pedal point on V, stationary in contrast to the moving bass of the A-section, suggests the contraposition of the dominant region to the tonic region. Additional connecting elements are the dotted rhythm of the upbeat, the frequent use of the suspension and the increasing sixteenth notes.

Op. 2/2–IV (m. 1–16) is another illustration of the practice form. The contrasting middle section is again on a pedal. The repetition of the two-measure unit is a slight variation.

In Op. 2/2–II (m. 1–19), the two-measure unit of the B-section (m. 9–12) is only slightly concealed by the imitation in the left hand. Otherwise, this case differs from the others only in the length of the recapitulation.

In all three, and in many of the following, the B-section ends on V, as an 'upbeat chord', and a small figure serves as a connective to the recapitulation.

In Op. 7–II the B-section and the A¹-section are longer than in the practice form. The length of the contrasting middle section is six measures (m. 9–14). This prolongation arises from a double repetition of its opening phrase, m. 9–10. The omission of one of the three units would reduce it to the four measures of the practice form. Curiously enough, any one of the three could equally well be omitted.

In the Rondo, Op. 2/2–IV, there is a second ternary form, the sections of which again deviate in length from the practice form. The A-section is ten measures, from the repeat mark in m. 57 to m. 66; the middle section is eight measures, m. 67–74. With the exception of the cadence, the B-section consists of a series of imitations of a two-measure unit, progressing along a circle of fourths.

The Rondo, Op. 7–IV, begins with the dominant harmony; the B-section, m. 9, can accordingly begin with the tonic. The contour of the A-section is essentially a descending scale line, which provokes ascending scale lines in the continuation.

The contrasting middle section of Op. 14/2–II consists again of a two-measure unit followed by a varied repetition. The relation to the A-section lies in the phrasing, while the contrast is emphasized by the legato style.

In Op. 26–I each section is double the usual length, and the middle section is even further extended. It consists of a sequentially repeated two-measure unit (m. 17–18), followed by a cadence. A deceptive progression (m. 24) produces the prolongation.

Op. 27/1–III. The 'con espressione' of the Adagio movement of this 'Sonata Quasi una Fantasia' is justified even by its construction. One might be inclined to question the coherence of the syncopations in m. 13–16. The syncopations in m. 9 are obviously a development of those in m. 6 and 7. But those in m. 13–16 present a special piano style, a variant of the more usual form in which the harmony, not the melody, is syncopated. This melodic outburst is not solely the result of exuberance. A great composer's imagination is not exhausted when he reaches the vicinity of a cadence. On the contrary, it often starts to bloom here, where lesser composers are happy to have arrived at a point where they can end. Ex. 101 illustrates that there was no formal necessity for the prolongation; a slight change in measure 12 would have made it possible to eliminate m. 13–16 entirely.

Op. 28–II. The contrasting middle section comprises eight measures, *dwelling on the dominant*. It consists of a pedal point on V, above which each reappearance of V is introduced by H. The section is prolonged by the progressively condensed repetition of measure 12, and an unaccompanied connective.

Op. 31/1–III. The middle section (m. 9–16) consists of the four measure-segment, m. 9–12, which is strictly repeated. Here the contrasting section starts with a pedal point on the tonic, and ends also on the tonic. This somewhat unusual procedure derives from the fact that the A-section (m. 1–8) and the recapitulation (m. 17–24) stand upon dominant pedal points. Thus the tonic offers sufficient contrast. The usual I–V relation between these two sections is reversed.

Illustrations from the literature: Haydn, Mozart, Schubert[1]

Haydn, Piano Sonata No. 35, Ex. 102a. The construction of the nine-measure middle section (m. 9–17) is interesting in that it consists of 2+4+2+1. The opening two-measure phrase (m. 9–10) is repeated (m. 11), sequenced (m. 12), varied (m. 13) and concluded with element 'b' (m. 14). The overlapping treatment produces a four-

---

[1] Most of these examples were selected because they differ, in all three sections, from the scheme of the practice form, thus indicating the great variety which is possible, even within so simple a basic structure.

measure unit of *chain-like construction*. The repetition of the last two measures of it (m. 15–16) emphasizes its end. M. 17 is an added connective.

Ex. 102*b*. The middle section begins (m. 11) with a stronger contrast than the dominant, the flat mediant (♭III). According to the principle of multiple meaning it is reinterpreted in m. 12 as III of the tonic minor, which then leads in m. 14 to the common dominant of the tonic major and minor. The extension of the A-section and the A¹-section by the addition of m. 8–9 and m. 22–23 constitutes another difference from the practice form.

Ex. 102*c*. The antecedent of the opening period (m. 1–12), becomes six measures long through repetitions of the motive-form 'b'. The alternative analysis, 'c', demonstrates the overlapping, chain-like, construction. The recapitulation (m. 17–22) is reduced to six measures. It uses chiefly the motive-form 'b', avoiding monotony by reorganization and by omitting the motive-form 'a', which was the exclusive material of the middle section.[1]

Ex. 102*d*. The motival derivation of the rich ornamentation, which might seem arbitrary at first glance, is analysed and traced back to a few basic forms.

Ex. 102*e*. The deceptive cadence in m. 8 of the A-section requires an added cadence to the dominant, which extends the section to ten measures. The recapitulation, partly (m. 23–24) a free reconstruction, becomes nine measures through the developing repetition in m. 22. The contrasting middle section (m. 11–17) dwells on the dominant of the tonic minor, partly as a pedal point. A mere interchange of harmonies (I–V; II–V) leads repeatedly to the dominant. In m. 13–17 the bass is omitted, on the supposition that the mind retains the pedal point—perhaps because the upper three voices express the harmony definitely enough. The extension to seven measures is the result of the inserted measure 13 and the additions, m. 16 and 17.

Ex. 103, by Mozart, possesses the simplicity and impressiveness so necessary in a theme for variations. It demonstrates that sufficient variety can be produced by means as simple as shifting to other harmonies, changing the intervals and extending the phrases to two measures. The elaboration through imitations, in the middle section, creates an excellent contrast to the homophonic style of the rest.

Ex. 104, Schubert. The contrasting middle section is noteworthy because it turns in m. 11 to the submediant region (vi) and ends on its V (III of the tonic region). This, in turn, influences the curious harmony at the beginning of the recapitulation, m. 13 (see explanation in Exs. 104*b*, *c*).

COMMENT ON EXAMPLES

Ex. 105 shows how ten different continuations can be derived from a single A-section. Though these B-sections begin on various degrees (V, i, v, ii, iii, III, IV, iv,

---

[1] This example can also be analysed as a baroque binary structure, in which the harmony moves from I to V in the first half and from V to I in the second; the motive-forms are similarly distributed in the two sections.

vi), all but one can be joined to the original A-section, ending on I. The basic phrase is a derivative of Ex. 21*d*.

Observe the various types of piano style and the treatment of the motive of the accompaniment (indicated by m, n, o, p). The features of the basic motive appearing in the A-section (marked a, b, c, d) are used subsequently, and combined with those of the motive of the accompaniment as logical connectives.

The upbeat chord at the end of all these B-sections is V, sometimes postponed to the last eighth or sixteenth.

In middle sections 1, 3, 7, 8 and 9 the minor tonic and minor subdominant are effectively contrasted with the ensuing return of the major in the recapitulation.

The harmonic procedure is sufficiently analysed in the examples themselves. The student should exploit, in like manner, all degrees, in order to expand his harmonic knowledge, even at the risk of overburdening so small a form. By this means, he can develop his harmonic resources and skill to meet the demands of larger and more complex forms.

THE UPBEAT CHORD

The B-section ends on a harmony which leads to the recapitulation. In classical music this harmony is the dominant, because it reintroduces the tonic in its tonality-defining sense. Its effect in such cases is comparable to that of an upbeat to the subsequently accentuated downbeat. Because of this function, such chords will be called 'upbeat chords', regardless of their rhythmic placement.

Other harmonies, and transformations of them, can also function as connectives. Ex. 106 shows examples of ii and iii (and their derivatives) used as upbeat harmonies to I. In Exs. 107*a*, *b* and *c*, the recapitulation does not begin on I. In such cases the upbeat chord must be chosen accordingly. In Ex. 107*b* the upbeat harmony is ♭III, introducing the recapitulation which begins on V. In Ex. 107*a* the recapitulation begins on ♯I, introduced by ♭VI. Of course, if the first two harmonies of the recapitulation were reversed, the ♭VI could as logically introduce I (Ex. 107*c*).

THE RECAPITULATION (A¹)

The recapitulation may be an unchanged repetition. More frequently it is changed, modified or varied. Changes may be necessary to establish a definite ending, especially if the A-section ends on a degree other than I. Shortening (by elimination, reduction or condensation) may help to avoid monotony. Lengthening (by insertion, interpolated repetitions, extension or addition) may create emphasis.

Modification of both melody and harmony may be necessary to accommodate such changes.

The principles of variation can be applied to all the elements of the A-section, but with moderation, so as not to conceal the presence of a repetition. Thus, the contour of the melody should not be entirely changed, except at points where essential structural changes occur. Ornamental variation—breaking down longer notes through the use of passing notes, circumscribing notes, tone repetitions, etc.—need not change the contour essentially. Excessive rhythmic changes or shifts of accent are likely to prevent recognition.

Variation of the harmony will consist largely of insertions and substitutions. The accompaniment may be varied by making changes in the figuration, though such changes should be less far-reaching than in the melody. Further variation can be produced by contrapuntal or semi-contrapuntal methods: imitation, addition of a counter melody or the melodic elaboration of subordinate voices.

A changed cadence may require considerable reformulation, or even complete reconstruction.

In a small form, alterations should be used with discretion, maintaining a balance with preceding sections.

Illustrations from the literature

Beethoven, Op. 2/1–II. The recapitulation of the initial ternary form is reduced to four measures. Only the first measure (m. 13) is preserved, an octave higher. M. 14 turns at once to IV, in preparation for the cadence. Connected by the rhythm of the upbeat to m. 1, which was omitted in approaching m. 13, m. 15 is a figuration of a descending contour resembling m. 3 and 7.

Op. 2/2–II. The seven-measure recapitulation (m. 13–19) combines reduction (omitting m. 3–5) and extension (by adding sequentially m. 15–16). M. 17 is an ascending reformulation of m. 6, through which the repetition of m. 7–8 (in m. 18–19) occurs climactically an octave higher. The sequences and the ascending contour of this reconstruction lend emphasis to the upper voice, which was previously somewhat obscured by the competing bass voice.

Op. 2/2–IV. The recapitulation of the first ternary form (m. 1–16) is reduced to four measures (m. 13–16) by melodic and harmonic condensations. In the second ternary form (m. 57–79), the recapitulation is reduced to five measures (m. 75–79), with a slight melodic variation.

Op. 7–II. The recapitulation (m. 15–24) is extended to ten measures. This is achieved by sequences and other repetitions, condensations and the deceptive cadence in m. 20, which requires a second, enriched cadence.

Op. 7–IV. The recapitulation (m. 13–16) repeats only the second half of the period, slightly varying the piano style by the addition of octaves.

Op. 14/2–II. The recapitulation is reduced to four measures (m. 13–16), followed by a codetta-like addition in the form of an enriched cadence.

Op. 26–I. The recapitulation (m. 27–34) repeats only the second half (m. 9–16) of the sixteen-measure period.

Op. 27/1, Adagio. The recapitulation (m. 17–24) repeats the entire A-section, with minor elaborations of the piano style, and a cadence changed to lead to the tonic.

Op. 28–II. The recapitulation (m. 17–22) omits m. 3–5, and condenses m. 6–8 into two measures (m. 21–22), converting the cadence to lead to the tonic. This reduction is balanced by the insertion of two semi-sequential repetitions of m. 18.

Op. 31/1–III. The recapitulation (m. 17–24) is noteworthy because the main melody is transferred to the tenor voice, while a quasi-melodically elaborated accompaniment is added in the right hand.[1]

Ex. 102b. The recapitulation (m. 15–24) omits the first four measures of the A-section. This reduction is again balanced by extending the content of the second half of this period to ten measures. This extension is produced by repetition of m. 17, followed by a dramatic pause, thus adding two measures. After this interruption the cadential measures follow, introduced by derivatives of the preceding figure. The last three measures are a mere transposition of m. 8–10 to the tonic.

Ex. 102c. Discussion of the recapitulation appears on p. 122.

Ex. 102d. In m. 13–17 of the recapitulation only the embellishments are varied. The cadence, m. 18–20, replacing the half-cadence to V with a full cadence to I, naturally requires more change.

Ex. 102e. The recapitulation was discussed on p. 122.

Ex. 104. The beginning of the recapitulation (m. 13) surprisingly makes use of the augmented 6/5 chord (on ♯) of the submediant region. Here it is treated as if it were a dominant seventh chord on IV, resolving to a diminished seventh chord derived from V. In view of the preceding cadence to the dominant of vi, it should probably be understood as in Exs. 104b and c.

The possibility that the recapitulation might begin on a different degree than the beginning was mentioned on p. 123, and is illustrated in Exs. 107a, b and c, in which the recapitulations begin, respectively, on ♯, V, and I 6/4. Such cases are comparatively rare in the small ternary form.

---

[1] Such a voice is often miscalled a 'counterpoint'. Real counterpoint is based on invertible combinations; but in homophonic music one more often finds the semi-contrapuntal technique of providing counter-melodies, repetition of imitative figures, etc., which vary the accompaniment to the main voice. A very enlightening instance is Beethoven's String Quartet, Op. 18/6, Adagio.

SMALL TERNARY FORM

Ex.101

Beethoven; Op.27/1- III

Ex.102

a) *Haydn,* Piano Sonata No.35- III

b) Piano Sonata No. 40-II

c) Piano Sonata, No. 28-III

d) Piano Sonata, No. 42-I

e) Piano Sonata No.48-I
Andante con espress.

Ex.103
Mozart, Sonata for Violin and Piano, K.V. 377-II

Ex.104
a) *Schubert*, String Quartet, Op 29-II

Ex.105

Meas. 13 of
Ex. 105a follows

Ex.106

Ex.107

a) *Schubert*, Waltzes, Op.9, No.32

tonic III   ♭VI   ♯I$^4_3$ I$^6_4$ V$_7$ I
minor

b) Op.9, No.33

tonic VII   III   V   I
minor

c) from Ex.107a

I$^6_4$ ♯I$^6_5$ V$_7$

XIV

UNEVEN, IRREGULAR AND
ASYMMETRICAL CONSTRUCTION

MANY of the previous illustrations from the literature demonstrate that a sentence or period may consist of an uneven number of measures. Their construction, accordingly, may be asymmetrical or irregular. The uneven number of measures may be caused by the length of basic units (motives or phrases), the number of such units, or the combination of units of differing lengths.

There are asymmetrical periods which are divided in unequal parts, for instance 4+6 (Exs. 45a, 47a, 59b, c, h). There are also symmetrical periods whose smaller segments are not divisible by four, e.g. 3+3 (Ex. 51e); 5+5 (Ex. 44a; 114); or 6+6 (Ex. 102c). Ex. 46e (5+7) is an asymmetrical period made up of uneven segments, but like all the preceding illustrations comprises an even number of measures.

Sentences are more frequently composed of elements of differing lengths than periods, even if the total number of measures is even. Ex. 57 is 4+5; Ex. 61c is also 4 (2+2)+5 (1+1+1+2). Ex. 61d is 5+4. Ex. 59i is made up of five units totalling seven measures (1+2+1+1+2).

In many cases the construction is complicated by the inclusion of internal repetitions, sequential or varied (Exs. 57, 59d, h, 60h, 61c); by stretching as in Exs. 44l and 47a, where a cadence that normally would occupy two measures is extended to three; or by additions after the cadence (Exs. 59c, 60a). In Ex. 59a, from the standpoint of melodic construction, there could be a cadence ending in m. 8, or, following the cadential harmonies of m. 9, a close in m. 10 or 11. But all these earlier opportunities are ingeniously evaded, thus extending the sentence to thirteen measures. Ex. 60f is constructed by internal repetitions of elements of differing lengths: 3(2+1)+3(2+1) +4(2+2)+2+2.

The extraordinary Brahms example, Ex. 51e, is a period of six measures. The antecedent and consequent (three measures long) each combine one 3/4 and two 2/4 measures. Nevertheless it is symmetrical and regular.

There exist forms which are built exclusively from phrases of an uneven length. For instance, the opening theme of the last movement of Brahms's Piano Quartet in g-minor is an A–B–A¹ form and consists of ten three-measure phrases. A phrase like these, consisting of six quarter-notes, may be understood as resembling one measure of 3/2, which demonstrates its naturalness (Ex. 108b). The same explanation applies to Ex. 108*a*, from Beethoven's *Harp* Quartet, Op. 74 (*si ha s'imaginar la battuta di* 6/8), and to Ex. 109 from the Scherzo of his Ninth Symphony (*ritmo di tre battute*). The *ritmo di tre battute*, instead of connecting two units (2+1 or 1+2), reduces the four measures of the *ritmo di quatro battute* to three (Ex. 110).

Irregular construction becomes more frequent in the second half of the nineteenth century. Brahms and Mahler, under the influence of folk music, developed a feeling that often led to free rhythmic organization which does not correspond to the bar lines (Ex. 111*a, b*). In extreme cases frequent changes of metre have been used to bring about a degree of correspondence between phrase structure and bar lines (Ex. 112).

Thus it becomes evident that master composers freely introduce irregular or non-symmetrical procedures as demanded by the musical idea or the structure. Often such procedures contribute fluency and spontaneity. But they are neither arbitrary nor casual. On the contrary, a high degree of skill and sensitivity are necessary to achieve the necessary balance and proportion.

Ex.108

a) *Beethoven*, String Quartet, Op.74-III

Si ha imaginar la battuta di $\frac{6}{8}$

etc.

b) *Brahms*, Piano Quartet, Op.25-IV Rondo alla Zingarese

Presto

Ex.109

Beethoven, Symphony No.9-II

Ritmo di tre battute

Ex.110

Beethoven, Symphony No.9-II

Ritmo di quattro battute

Ex. 111

a) *Brahms,* String Quartet, Op. 51/2-II

b) *Schoenberg,* String Quartet, Op.7

Ex. 112

Bartók, String Quartet No.3

XV

THE MINUET

Minuet, scherzo, theme and variation, etc., appear as independent pieces, or as middle movements in cyclic forms such as the suite, symphony or sonata.

The only specific rhythmic feature of a minuet is the metre, 3/4 (or, rarely, 3/8). Striking rhythms, like those in scherzos or more modern dances, are seldom found. Beethoven marks the Minuet of the First Symphony, $\downarrow$. = 108, and that of the Eighth Symphony, $\downarrow$ = 126. Both tempi are extreme, even for Beethoven. Most of his other minuets, and those of Mozart and Haydn, average about $\downarrow$. = 60–70, though some are as slow as $\downarrow$. = 40–50. Accordingly, more small note values (eighths and sixteenths) appear in the minuet, and the harmony changes more frequently than in the scherzo. In other dance forms, the harmony often remains unchanged for a number of measures; in the minuet the harmony seldom lasts longer than one or two measures, and often there are two or more harmonies within a measure.

The character of a minuet may range from the unpretentiously singable (e.g. Beethoven, Op. 31/3–III) to the stubbornly insistent (Mozart, Symphony No. 40 in g-minor); but in general the character, like the tempo, is moderate.

As the minuet was the favoured dance of the courts in the eighteenth century, it did not call for so much accentuation of the rhythm as did the more popular dances. Accordingly, the conventional accompaniments (cf. Ex. 65) were probably never much used. If some vestiges of them appear, they are generally stylized.

THE FORM

The minuet is an A–B–A¹ form, quite similar to the small ternary form. A practice form derived from it need not deviate from this A–B–A¹. However, the fact that the B-section must, because of the customary repetition marks (‖: A: ‖: B A¹: ‖), follow first the A-section and then the A¹-section, has to be taken into consideration. Ex. 113, by Bach, is an illustration of the simple minuet, and corresponds quite closely to the practice form.

Many minuets in the literature differ from the practice form. There are structural deviations in all the three parts: unequal length of phrases; sequential or other internal repetitions; extensions (often provoked by deceptive progressions); or codettas added to the A-section and its recapitulation. Mozart and Haydn, especially, often insert episodes; and even co-ordinate ideas appear, sometimes only rudimentary, but occasionally quite independent and firmly established.

The recapitulation is seldom shortened, and seldom reveals far-reaching changes of the melodic contour. It is usually linked with the B-section by an upbeat chord. This upbeat chord (dominant, artificial dominant, etc.) is frequently reinforced by dwelling upon it, often over a pedal point. Sometimes a small connective is added.

Illustrations from the literature

Haydn and Mozart built many themes of minuets of an uneven number of measures. In Ex. 114 the A-section is a period of ten measures (5+5). In the recapitulation it is repeated without change, and a ten-measure added section (codetta) is built from a one-measure rest and nine measures of content.

Haydn, String Quartet, Op. 76/2–III (Ex. 115). The A–section of the Minuet consists of 5+6 measures, but it might also be analysed as 4+4+3. This ambiguity is due to the canonic imitation, which shifts the ending of the first segment to the fifth measure.

Although many movements in the classic literature combine the homophonic and the contrapuntal technique, there is a fundamental difference between them. The homophonic-melodic treatment depends basically on development of a motive by variation. In contrast, the contrapuntal treatment does not vary the motive, but displays the possibilities of combination inherent in the basic theme or themes.

The Minuet in Mozart's String Quartet in A, K.V. 464 (Ex. 116), is a rare example of the real fusion of the two techniques. The three motives, A, B and C, can all be considered circumscriptions of a fourth (see Ex. 117). The two principal subjects, A and B, admit canonic imitations and inversions; they even appear simultaneously with their inversions. Their combination appears in prime, octave and lower sixth. In measure 59–60 the combination is inverted in the upper seventh, and B accompanies A in canonic imitation. In the contrasting middle section a sequence of B is accompanied by the interval of a fourth, which (Ex. 117) can be derived from both A and B by reduction.

Beside the display of contrapuntal values, one finds also the usual variation of basic motives (m. 22–24); and there is even a codetta (m. 25–28).

Beethoven, Op. 2/1–III. The rather distantly related motive form in m. 11–12, and its repetition (m. 13–14) may be considered the consequence of many repetitions within the A-section. The sequential modulation in the contrasting middle section leads to the subdominant with the previously mentioned motive-form (m. 20). In m. 23 and 24 it is reduced (liquidated) to three notes, which are then reassembled in a chain of eighth notes moving to the dominant. The A¹-section is a reformulation, omitting entirely the content of m. 3–4.

Op. 10/3–III. The contrasting middle section is built from a two-measure phrase (m. 17–18) which is a remote derivation from the A-section (see Ex. 118). It makes four appearances, moving in a circle of fifths (iii–vi–II–V). The structural reformulation of the A¹-section does not involve the antecedent, which is merely a 'reinstrumentation' (m. 25–32). The consequent is lengthened by the insertion of a climactic sequence introducing the cadential subdominant; its ending (m. 43) is approached through a number of passing harmonies. Several codettas conclude the Minuet.

Op. 22–III. The trill-like segment (m. 9, 13) of the contrasting middle section can be derived from the first three eighth-notes in the left hand of m. 2, under the influence of the sixteenth-notes throughout the A-section. The phrase, m. 11–12, derives from the beginning phrase, from which all of the A-section is derived (Ex. 119). The recapitulation, substantially unvaried, is concluded by several codettas.

The contrasting middle sections of these three, and many other, minuets resemble the elaboration (development, *Durchführung*) to be discussed under the Scherzo. In these, and in some movements not specifically called Minuets (Op. 7–III, Op. 27/2–II), the chief characteristic is the sequential modulation. The end of the section is often marked by dwelling on the dominant over a pedal point. The pedal point is a retarding device. It should be employed where the harmony must be prevented from too rapid or too distant development. Usually the sustained note is in the bass, and the upper voices carry out a progression from V to V.

For the recapitulation (A¹-section), the same principles discussed in the chapter on the Small Ternary Form apply. Since Mozart, it has become almost a *point d'honneur* not to use an unvaried repetition, but to reformulate and reconstruct. Such a case is the Minuet from Mozart's String Quartet in *A*, K.V. 464, quoted in Ex. 116.

The preservation of the rhythmic features is so strong a motive relation that it allows far-reaching variations of the intervals and the contour without producing incoherence. In Ex. 116 the recapitulation is quite obvious (m. 55) in spite of such melodic reconstruction.

THE TRIO

Most of the dance forms are followed by a trio, and it is usual after the trio to repeat the original dance. As a matter of fact, the trio is nothing else than a second minuet (march, waltz, scherzo; or—as in the suites of Bach—a second courante, bouree or gavotte).

It is evident that this trio has to constitute a contrast. One assumes that there should also be some thematic connexion. In former times the trio was either in the same tonality, or in the relation *maggiore-minore* (tonic major—tonic minor), or vice versa. Later the contrast between relative major and minor was also used, as well as between other pairs of related keys.

The contrast in character might be, e.g. lyrical—rhythmical; melodious—contrapuntal; melodious—étude-like; grazioso—energico; dolce—vivace; melancholy—gay; et cetera and vice versa.

Concerning the form, there may appear as many deviations in the trio as in the minuet itself: reductions, extensions, additional ideas, codettas, etc.

MINUETS

Ex. 113
Bach, French Suite No. 6 - Menuetto

Ex. 114
Haydn, String Quartet, Op. 54/1- Menuetto

Ex. 115
Haydn, String Quartet, Op.76/2 - III

Ex. 116
Mozart, String Quartet, K.V. 464 - Menuetto

N.B. Compass of each motive is a 4th

canonic imitation

Ex. 117

Ex.118

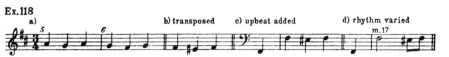

Ex.119

XVI

THE SCHERZO

SCHERZO, according to Webster, means a 'playful, humorous movement, commonly in 3/4 measure, which, since Beethoven, usually takes the place of the old minuet in a sonata or symphony'. This is only partly correct. For instance, Beethoven's Septet, Op. 20, symphonic in its first and last movements, contains both a Minuet and a Scherzo.

Any attempt to define the structure of the scherzo strictly will meet similar problems. Beethoven seldom uses the title, Scherzo, if the movement, like that of the String Trio, Op. 9/3, is in minor. To this degree it is true that his scherzos may be called playful, humorous, gay. But among eight scherzos from Brahms's chamber music, five are in minor. Beethoven calls 'Scherzo' only two of the rapid middle movements of his symphonies. Many such movements in his sonatas and string quartets are only labelled Allegro, Vivace, Presto, etc., probably because of deviations in character, form, mode, rhythm, tempo or metre, from the strict concept that he had in mind. Among these movements can be found some in minor and some in metres other than 3/4, e.g. 3/8, 6/8, 6/4, 2/2, 4/4, 2/4, etc. The structure of the B-section also varies considerably. Schubert's scherzos are mostly in triple metre, but often in minor. In Brahms, Schumann and Mendelssohn one finds many different metres.

With regard to character and mood, the restriction to the playful and humorous is not factual. Even the tempo is not decisive. Beethoven's own metronome indications for rapid middle movements range around $\downarrow$. = 100, which is his average scherzo tempo. However, these middle movements, with only the rapid tempo in common, differ very widely in expressive qualities.

A survey of scherzos and other rapid middle movements of Beethoven, Schubert, Mendelssohn, Schumann, Chopin, Brahms, Tchaikovsky, Berlioz, Bruckner, Mahler, Reger, Debussy, Ravel, etc., reveals such characters as: vivacious, sparkling, brilliant, witty, enthusiastic, ecstatic, ardent, fiery, energetic, vehement, impassioned, dramatic, tragic, heroic, gigantesque, diabolical, grotesque.

The scherzo is distinctly an instrumental piece, characterized by rhythmical accentuations, and rapid tempo. The tempo prevents frequent change of the harmonies and remote variation of motive-forms.

With regard to structure, scherzos of the masters have only one thing in common, they are *ternary forms*. They differ from smaller ternary forms and the minuet in that the middle section is more modulatory and more thematic. In some cases, there is a special type of *modulatory contrasting middle section* which approaches the elaboration (*Durchführung*)[1] of the Sonata Allegro.

THE A-SECTION

In principle, the A-section does not differ from the A-sections which were previously discussed. Often the theme is double the usual number of measures on account of the rapid tempo. For example, the Scherzos of Op. 2/2, Op. 2/3, Op. 28, and the Second Symphony (Ex. 120c) begin with periods. The Scherzos of the Violin Sonata, Op. 30/2 (Ex. 120a), the String Quartet, Op. 18/1 (Ex. 120b), and the *Eroica* Symphony (Ex. 121a) begin with sentences.

The character of the last of these has had great influence as the model for many subsequent scherzos. Structurally (as the analysis in Ex. 121d shows) it is a circumscription of the ascending tonic and the descending dominant (Exs. 121b, c). This skeleton is clothed with auxiliaries and passing notes. The relation between this theme and those of the first and fourth movements (Exs. 121d, e) is strong evidence in favour of the concept of 'monothematicism' in a cyclic work.

THE MODULATORY CONTRASTING MIDDLE SECTION

The main function of the B-section is to provide contrast. It is generally held that the B-section of a scherzo should be an elaboration (*Durchführung*). But in fact it often resembles the B-section of the minuet, while many minuets possess a modulatory contrast.

The A-section, over relatively stable harmony, exposes its motive-forms in various aspects. In the modulatory middle section, changes of shape and even of constitution occur as this same material passes through fluctuating, unstable harmonic situations. This freedom of structure and motive treatment does not imply that regularity, logic and balance can be ignored.

Again, it is advisable to become acquainted with this new type of contrast through practice form, which, like all abstractions, differs from reality, and replaces freedom with guiding restrictions.

THE PRACTICE FORM

The modulation must be organized to promote intelligibility. Therefore, it should proceed, not in one great leap, but gradually, according to a plan which provides for

---

[1] The terms 'elaboration' and *Durchführung* are used interchangeably throughout this book to refer to the technique odinarily called 'development', and to the sections of larger forms which make extensive use of this technique. Schoenberg rejected the more usual term on the grounds that little development (in the sense of growth, maturation, evolution) takes place in the material used. Motive-forms are adapted, varied, expanded, condensed, recombined and carried through various keys or regions; but they seldom grow or evolve into a 'more mature or advanced state' (Ed.).

returning to the tonic. It is also advisable to provide for repetitions of clearly delimited segments, reasonable in length.

Harmonically, these segments should be built as patterns for sequences. Thematically, they should possess a certain degree of independence; the combination of motive-forms may resemble that in the antecedent of the period, or the middle section of the ternary form. But motive-forms from the A-section will have to be modified or adapted to the modulatory procedure. The order may be changed, and some of the forms may be repeated within the segment (e.g. *abac, abcc, abbc, aaab*, etc.). Because of the modulation, remotely varied motive-forms are dangerous.

In the practice form the pattern is followed by a sequence. It should begin on a degree related to the ending of the A-section. In Ex. 122 there are twenty-five illustrations of patterns with sequences, all derived from the A-section shown. They begin on various degrees, such as V, v, III, I, iii, ♭III, ii, iv, VI, etc. The patterns of Exs 122*b, c* and *d* begin alike but continue differently. In a number of cases different sequences are given for the same pattern. Variation of the sequence is illustrated in Exs. 122*r, s, t, u, v, x* and *y*. Particularly noteworthy are those in which the principal voice shifts to a different voice, sometimes using the opportunities of double counterpoint.

In order to control the modulation, the pattern must be built so that the end of the last sequence offers an opening for the return to an appropriate upbeat harmony preparing for the recapitulation. For instance, the sixteenth measure of Exs. 122*l* and *m* are too remote to be neutralized through simple procedures.

The emphasis contributed by a sequence (a form of repetition) creates obligations. It is necessary to neutralize these obligations in order to introduce the recapitulation in a manner at once 'surprising and expected', as Beethoven expressed it.

This is accomplished by the technique of *liquidation*, i.e. by gradually depriving the motive-forms of their characteristic features and dissolving them into uncharacteristic forms, such as scales, broken chords, etc. A striking example is the Scherzo of Beethoven's Op. 26. After the sequence, the four-measure pattern is reduced to two (m. 25–26); after a varied repetition, it is further reduced to five notes (m. 28); to four notes (m. 29–30); to two notes (m. 33 ff.); and to one note (m. 41 ff. Observe that the upbeat harmony is reached at the beginning of the first reduction (m. 25) and continued through m. 44.

If, in the practice form, the end of the sequence does not connect readily with the upbeat harmony, further modulation is necessary. This can be accomplished through additional sequences, but in order to start the liquidation, the pattern should be reduced, ordinarily to half of the previous length.

In Ex. 122 various techniques of continuation after the first sequence are illustrated. In Ex. 122*a* the reduced pattern is made simply by omitting the third and fourth measures of the original pattern. The contour of the pattern (m. 9–12) has been depreciated into the inconspicuous form of a descending scale line. Such unpretentious forms as scale lines, broken chords, and the like, are neutral enough to cancel the emphasis of the sequential process. M. 25–29 dwell on the dominant, with an ostinato-like treatment of residues.

The brackets in m. 21 ff. of Exs. 122*b*, *c* and *d* indicate the reduction of the preceding two-measure pattern to two notes.

The end of the liquidation is generally marked by a combination of repose and suspense: repose through cessation of the modulatory movement; suspense in anticipation of the re-entrance of the theme. At this point, the retarding effect of a pedal point is appropriate; it keeps at least the bass from progressing. As an inverted pedal, it can also be a sustained or repeated note in another voice. The pedal can be developed into a pedal figure (in Ex. 122*f*, m. 20–22, all three upper voices participate in such an ostinato-like formulation). In Ex. 122*d*, m. 17–21, part of the modulation is carried out similarly.

Illustrations from the literature

Most of the scherzos and scherzo-like movements in classic music have in common only one feature, that the modulation is carried out at least in part by sequential treatment. The following are particularly worth study: *Beethoven*: Piano sonatas, Op. 2/2, Op. 2/3, Op. 26, Op. 28; Septet, Op. 20; Symphonies 1, 2, 4, 7, 9; String Quartets, Op. 18/1, Op. 18/2, Op. 18/6; *Brahms*: Sextets, Op. 18, Op. 36.

In some cases, the modulation is interrupted by an episode which settles down for a time, often at a point harmonically remote (e.g. Op. 2/2, Symphony II). A remodulation follows, using residues or other derivatives.

As soon as the upbeat harmony is reached, further modulation or remodulation becomes unnecessary, as in Op. 26, where the shortened segment already stands on the upbeat harmony.

Op. 28, Scherzo. The contrasting middle section does not contain a real modulation, but merely passes through a number of harmonies with the aid of artificial dominants. Even the upbeat chord is introduced in an unusual manner and in the imperfect form of a 6/5 chord. The adequacy of this contrast is based on the harmonic peculiarities of the other sections and the trio. The ambiguity of the opening *f♯* (most strongly felt after the *b* minor of the trio) requires a clear definition of the tonic, *D*. After several more or less contradictory deviations, the tonality becomes firmly established only at the end of the recapitulation, with the aid of several codettas.

Motivally, the construction of this middle section depends on the sustained *D*, *E*, *F♯*, *G* in the upper voice, each four measures long, like the initial *F♯*; and the octave leaps in the bass. Below these sustained notes, the bass, accompanied by upper thirds, proceeds chromatically from *F♯* to *C♯*. The regularity of this procedure makes a motive-like impression.

Symphony No. 1–III, Menuetto. Although this movement is called a minuet, the contrasting middle section, in its sequentiation and gradual liquidation, resembles the practice form of the scherzo middle section. In contrast, the Scherzo of Symphony No. 2 has little elaboration of this type.

Symphony No. 3, Scherzo. The first ten measures of the *Durchführung* utilize the motive-forms of m. 1–4 in a chromatic ascension to reach the supertonic. Here the second element of the theme (m. 7–14) is quoted. The last four measures (m. 95–98) are split off and sequenced, modulating to V of the mediant, which, curiously, is dwelt upon for sixteen measures, as if it were the upbeat chord. Four measures of $B\flat$, representing the dominant, substitute for an upbeat chord.

Symphony No. 4–III. The modulation is carried out by means of many sequences of a four-measure pattern, which is liquidated by reduction to two measures, one measure and finally to two-thirds of a measure.

Symphony No. 7–III. This movement is scherzo-like in character, tempo and *Durch-führung*. The modulation follows the circle of fifths from mediant major to sub-dominant. At this point one of those 'recapitulations in the wrong key' occurs which appear occasionally in Beethoven's later works.

String Quartet, Op. 18/1, Scherzo. A three-measure pattern (in flat mediant) is sequenced in tonic minor. A two-measure pattern (m. 17) followed by three sequences leads to the dominant.

String Quartet, Op. 18/2, Scherzo. The contrast is chiefly harmonic, without elaboration of the basic motive.

String Quartet, Op. 18/6, Scherzo. The contrasting section remains substantially in the tonic region, but somewhat elaborates the basic motive.

Brahms, Sextet, Op. 18, Scherzo. Here the contrast is not produced by sequences, but by fluently passing through tonic minor and flat submediant major regions. The elaboration is carried out exclusively with imitations of the leading motive.

Brahms, Sextet, Op. 36, Scherzo. The elaboration is organized in imitative sequences, distributed as a dialogue between upper and lower voices.

These illustrations show the inexhaustible diversity of construction. They also show that there is such a wide latitude for the fantasy of the composer that only a trained mind can control it. Hence, composition in the practice form must be supplemented with analysis of master works.

THE RECAPITULATION

Disregarding literal repetition, the recapitulation may be changed, modified, varied or reconstructed as described on p. 123.

Op. 2/3, Scherzo. The recapitulation is modified so that both antecedent and consequent end on the tonic.

Op. 26, Scherzo. The recapitulation is enriched by the addition of a counter melody in the right hand; the principal melody is lowered an octave, appearing in the left hand. The written-out repetition, which was varied in the A-section, by the addition of passing notes, is varied in the recapitulation by interchange of the voices (m. 53–60), as in double counterpoint.

The A¹-section of many scherzos differs from the A-section in including extensions of the recapitulation, episodes and added codettas.

EXTENSIONS, EPISODES AND CODETTAS

Extension is usually produced by repetition (often sequential) of an element. In simple cases it is associated with a turn toward the subdominant (e.g. Beethoven, Symphony No. 1–III); in others a real modulation occurs. Motivally, if it is not the simple repetition of a segment (as in the Septet, Op. 20), it usually consists of a developing elaboration of preceding motive-forms.

Episodes interrupt the normal flow of a section. They dwell upon such progressions as neither modulate nor produce a cadence. They often settle down in a more or less remote contrasting region, especially if within a modulatory section. They often introduce small phrases, strangely foreign to the previously used motive-forms (e.g. Op. 2/2–III, m. 19 ff., discussed below).

Codettas are primarily cadences. They serve as reaffirmations of the ending of a section. Harmonically, they may consist of the most rudimentary cadence, V–I; or they may be highly complex. Motivally, they may range from simple repetitions of small elements to rather independent formulations.[1]

Further illustrations from the literature

Op. 2/2, Scherzo. An episode which is both motivally and harmonically remote begins in m. 19. It is connected with the basic material merely by its upbeat, which is related to the tone repetitions of m. 3. The remoteness of the region makes a relatively long and rapid remodulation necessary. A simple codetta at the end provides the full cadence which was missing in the recapitulation proper.

Op. 2/3, Scherzo. The codettas (m. 56–64) hint at the subdominant minor, and become plagal in the liquidated form, m. 61.

Op. 26, Scherzo. The recapitulation is extended with two slightly varied repetitions of the last two-measure phrase (m. 59–60), and brought to a close with liquidating reductions.

String Quartet, Op. 18/1, Scherzo. The A¹-section consists of an extended recapitulation (the extension is in m. 43–46), followed by an episode (m. 51–63) built from the element which appears in m. 49–50. The first five measures of the recapitula-

---

[1] Usually, if more than one codetta appears, the later ones are shortened, often in the manner of a liquidation.

tion are again repeated (m. 64–68) and then liquidated into scale lines (m. 70–78). A codetta, repeated and liquidated, concludes the movement.

String Quartet, Op. 18/2, Scherzo. The A¹-section contains an extended recapitulation. An enriched cadence starts in m. 22, within which, paradoxically, the end (m. 27–30), looks like a transposition of the beginning. There follows a codetta of four measures, motivally remote, which is repeated, interchanging the position of the parts as in multiple counterpoint. A smaller codetta (m. 38–39), repeated and liquidated, brings the movement to an end.

String Quartet, Op. 18/6, Scherzo. A codetta begins in m. 30, featuring closely related motive-forms. After frequent repetitions, the rhythm is condensed to equal eighth-notes in m. 39, which are finally liquidated into scale lines and broken chords.

String Quartet, Op. 59/2, Allegretto. In m. 17 the harmony settles down in a way that suggests the beginning of an episode, although it can also be interpreted as a kind of sequence of the preceding four measures. The segment, m. 21–28, repeated in m. 29–36 (where it overlaps the beginning of the recapitulation, m. 36) possesses the independence of an episode, but functions here as a remodulation (Neapolitan triad, followed by V and I). The A-section ends on VII (the subtonic of e minor). Hence, the recapitulation is changed considerably and its ending reaffirmed with added codettas. The last of these (m. 48–49), an augmentation of m. 47, can be considered as a written-out ritardando, such as performers conventionally supply to make the ending of a piece distinct.

String Quartet, Op. 74 (*Harp* Quartet), Presto. In m. 17 a long episode in the Neapolitan region begins. Its partial repetition remodulates. The recapitulation (m. 37) quotes only three measures of the beginning, and continues with a liquidating form of m. 3 to another episode on a pedal G (m. 43). This is partly repeated on a pedal C (m. 51). A series of codettas follows, but the usual form of the cadence is avoided. One may venture the hypothesis that this is intentional to provide an opening for the transition (m. 423) which connects this movement with the last movement.

Symphonies Nos. 1, 2 and 4 also exhibit extensions in the recapitulation, and codettas. The last codetta in the Scherzo of the Second Symphony is augmented, like a ritardando.

Symphony No. 3, Scherzo. The recapitulation, besides an extension, has a very long coda section (beginning in m. 115) comprising fifty-two measures, which elaborates and liquidates two codetta-like segments.

Brahms, Sextet, Op. 18, Scherzo. In the recapitulation, the twelve measures of the A-section are extended to eighteen by stubbornly repeating a circumscribing figure while the harmony changes below it.

Brahms, Sextet, Op. 36, Scherzo. The subdominant flavour of the A-section perhaps accounts for the deceptive use of a long ostinato around the G (I), and the false

recapitulation beginning in m. 56 or 57. The real recapitulation (m. 69) is introduced
by the very remote minor triad on F♯. It is concluded by three groups of codettas.

THE CODA

In larger forms even a considerable number of codettas may not be sufficient to
counterbalance all the preceding harmonic movement. Though this is seldom the case
in the scherzo, nevertheless short coda sections are often found in classical scherzos.
They consist of a number of codettas or codetta-like segments, occasionally modulatory, but always returning to the tonic. Generally, the later ones are progressively
shortened, in a liquidating manner, even to the smallest residues.

A more detailed discussion will be found in Chapter XVIII.

THE TRIO

The relation between scherzo and trio is the same as that between minuet and trio.

In many cases, the repetition of the scherzo follows a complete ending of the trio.
In other cases the recapitulation of the trio is liquidated into a transition, introducing
an upbeat chord for the repetition of the scherzo (Op. 2/3; String Quartet, Op. 18/1;
Fifth Symphony, m. 224–35). Often a little segment may be inserted between trio and
scherzo. In Op. 26 and the String Quartet, Op. 18/2, the motive of the scherzo is
reintroduced on modulatory harmony. A similar segment in Beethoven's Seventh
Symphony (m. 221–234) sounds like a little reminiscence of the trio. In the last two
measures (m. 235–6) a transposition of the motive reintroduces F.

The little segment in tonic minor in the String Quartet, Op. 18/6 (m. 65–68) is a
peculiar way of producing a slight contrast between the trio and scherzo, both in B♭
major. It is questionable whether this contrast of tonality is adequate, but recognition
of the need for such contrast is important.

The Scherzo of Brahms's Second Sextet, Op. 36, presents an extraordinary example
of mediation between two apparently heterogeneous themes. In m. 227, twenty-four
measures before the repetition of the scherzo in 2/4, a segment of eight measures
appears (Ex. 123a), whose foresentence is a reduction of the preceding measures,
which conclude the recapitulation of the trio (Ex. 123b). The analysis shows the
derivation of m. 5–8 from the trio melody; while m. 1–4 distinctly prepare for the
first phrase of the scherzo. Moreover, the construction of m. 1–4, in twos and fours,
may be considered a preparation for the return of 2/4. The passage ends in a written-
out ritardando, using the first notes of the ensuing scherzo.

Scherzo movements are often enlarged to the dimensions of a rondo. In the String
Quartets, Op. 74 and Op. 95, and Symphonies 4 and 7, Beethoven interpolates the
trio twice, alternating with three appearances of the scherzo. Schumann, in extension
of this idea, introduces two different trios (Piano Quintet, Op. 44).

SCHERZOS

Ex. 120

a) *Beethoven,* Violin Sonata, Op. 30/2 - III

b) String Quartet, Op. 18/1 - III

c) Symphony No. 2 - III

Ex. 121

a) Symphony No. 3 - III

Ex.122

b) Elaboration 2

c) Elaboration 3

Pattern   Sequence

liquidation   Reduced to two notes

Reduced pattern   Sequence

Broken chord   Recap.

d) Elaboration 4

Pattern   Sequence

ostinato-like

etc.

n) Sequence 14

o) Sequence 15

p) Sequence 16

q) Sequence 17

r) Sequence 18

melody shifted to inner voice

s) Sequence 19

condensation, liquidation

t) Sequence 20

u) Sequence 21 *

upper thirds omitted; varied

thirds added

v) Sequence 22 *

lower thirds omitted; varied

thirds added

* not actually sequence; parts inverted instead

w) Sequence 23 (cf. 19)

x) Sequence 24

y) Sequence 25

iii

Ex. 123

Brahms, Sextet Op. 36-II

Scherzo, Presto giocoso

a) m. 227

b) m. 225

End of Trio   Trio Theme (m. 221 f.)

XVII

THEME AND VARIATIONS

MUSICAL terminology is often ambiguous. This is due primarily to the origin of most of the terms: they are borrowed from other fields, such as poetry, architecture, painting and aesthetics. Terms like metre, symmetry, colour and balance are typical. But even worse is the use of single terms, like 'inversion', for several different things. One speaks of the first or second 'inversion' of a triad; the 'inversion' of an interval; mirror-like 'inversion', vertical and horizontal; contrapuntal 'inversion', as in multiple counterpoint.

Similarly, the term 'variation' has a number of meanings. Variation creates the motive-forms for the construction of themes. It produces contrast in middle sections, and variety in repetitions. But in 'Theme and Variations' it is the structural principle for a whole piece.

Production of an entire piece merely through the application of variation is an approach to the logic of larger compositions.

As the name indicates, the piece consists of a THEME and several VARIATIONS upon it. The number of variations is determined by whether it is a movement in a cyclic work, like Op. 26-I, Op. 14/2-II, Op. 111-II; or an independent piece like the *32 Variations in c minor*, or the *33 Diabelli Variations*, Op. 120. A middle movement in a cyclic work includes a lesser number of variations. Often the piece is concluded by a coda, finale or fugue. In other cases the last variation is extended; and sometimes there is no special ending after the last variation.

STRUCTURAL CONSTITUTION OF THE THEME

There are themes which facilitate, and others which impede, the production of variations. Variations are primarily repetitions, which would become intolerable without constant restimulation of the listener's interest. If the theme contains too many and too interesting features, there remains little scope for the additions which a simple theme readily permits.

Many classical variations are based on popular or folk melodies of the time. But such variations as Bach's *Goldberg Variations*; Beethoven's Op. 35, and the *32 Variations*; Brahms's String Quartet, Op. 67-IV and many others are based on the composer's own theme.

A simple theme will consist of closely related motive-forms, in preference to distant ones (Op. 14/2-II). Structurally, the theme should show definite subdivision and clear phrasing. One usually finds binary or ternary forms. The *12 Variations in A*, the *24 Variations in D*, and Op. 111–II, for example, are binary.[1] Op. 14/2–II and Op. 26–I are ternary. An exceptional case is the passacaglia-like theme, a sentence of eight measures, of the *32 Variations in c*.

The harmony should be simple, and should not change too frequently or too irregularly. See, for example, Beethoven's *15 Variations in E♭*, Op. 35; *Diabelli Variations*, Op. 120; *12 Variations in A*; *24 Variations in D*; *6 Variations in G*; *6 Easy Variations in G*. Except for the cadential segment, none of these themes contains more than two harmonies to a measure. In Op. 35 there is one harmony per measure; in the *A Variations* there are two; and in the *D and G Variations* there are three harmonies to two measures. But in the first eight measures of the *Diabelli* Waltz, the harmony changes only once. The use of mere interchange of I and V contributes to the simplicity of many of these themes.

The harmony of the *6 Variations in G*, though simple, is characteristic, especially because of the sequence in the middle section. The same procedure, among others, contributes to the memorability of the theme of Op. 26–I.

Even a master like Beethoven did not make many variations when the theme was long or complicated as, for instance, in the *6 Variations in F*, Op. 34; and perhaps also in Op. 14/2–II.

A unifying accompaniment facilitates variation, while one which changes too much can be a handicap. For this reason Beethoven, in the *9 Variations on a March of Dressler*, makes no other change in the first variation than the substitution of a unifying accompaniment.

It is not easy to write a good original theme for variation. It may, therefore, be useful to select a theme whose suitability has already been proved, in sets of variations by such masters as Haydn, Mozart and Beethoven.

RELATION BETWEEN THEME AND VARIATIONS

The form originated, perhaps, in the custom of repeating a pleasant theme several times, avoiding a decline of interest by introducing embellishments and other additions. This may be why the classic masters made it a point that the theme should be recognizable in the variation.

Thus the course of events should not be changed, even if the character is changed; the number and order of the segments remains the same. Sometimes the metre is changed, the tempo is changed or the number of measures is systematically multiplied

---

[1] This type of theme structure is characterized by two balanced segments, built from closely related but differentiated motive-forms, so that the second section is in some respects a contrast. Generally the first segment ends on the dominant; the second begins in the dominant (or other closely related) region, and closes with a cadence to I.

The difference between this structure and the small ternary form may consist in the absence of a real motival contrast (*12 Variations in A*); or in the absence of an identifiable repetition (*24 Variations in D*).

by two or three. But, in general, the proportions and structural relations of the parts, and the main features, are preserved. Of course, the viewpoint as to which constitute the main features is subject to change. Every variation should possess the same quality of formal self-sufficiency and coherence as the theme itself.

THE MOTIVE OF VARIATION

In classical music every variation shows a unity which surpasses that of the theme. It results from the systematic application of a *motive of variation*. In higher forms the motive derives from the theme itself, thus connecting all the variations intimately with the theme.

In the practice form the motive should consist of a predetermined figure, modified no more than accommodation to the harmony and structure requires (see, for example, the first eleven of the *Variations in c minor*).

PRODUCTION OF THE MOTIVE OF VARIATION

In order to arrive at a suitable motive of variation, it is necessary to recognize the essentials of the theme. Simplification by omission of everything which can be considered subordinate (e.g. embellishments, grace notes, passing notes, suspensions, appoggiaturas, trills, runs, etc.) unveils the basic construction. In making this reduction the relation to the harmony must be taken into consideration (see Exs. 124a, 126a). The simultaneous rhythmic simplification sometimes requires regularization, as in the last four measures of Ex. 124a, where some features have to be shifted to other beats. Since the viewpoint determining what features are essential is not necessarily uniform for all variations, there may be more than one usable 'skeleton'.

Since the motive of variation must be adaptable to the chosen 'skeleton', its nature and length will be limited by the number and distribution of the principal tones and harmonies. It will scarcely be longer than two measures; in many cases it is a half-measure or even less.

Variation around the principal tones. In the motives for at least the first few variations, it is common practice to circumscribe the principal tones with neighbouring tones. Often tones of the theme are included in parts of scale lines or broken chords. Of course, such elements must fit the expressed harmony. The rhythmic organization of the motive of variation has a great deal to do with its character. It is normally maintained consistently throughout the variation.

Illustrations from the literature

Beethoven, *Diabelli Variations*. A considerable number of the variations (2, 9, 11, 12, 14, 18, 28, for example) derive the motive of variation from more or less elaborate circumscription of the principal tones. Examples 124b, c and d show some of these cases in relation to the skeleton of Ex. 124*a*. Observe the rhythmic displacement of the principal tones.

Beethoven, *32 Variations in c minor*. The figure in sixteenth-notes of the first three variations is a combination of a broken chord with tone repetitions, the latter derived from the repeated *G* of the first three measures of the theme. The rhythmicization of the harmony in the first two variations also contributes to the motive of variation. Exs. 125*a* and *b* show the derivation of the motives of variation for Variations 4 and 5. In Variation 5, note the exchanged positions of *C* and *E♭*, an exchange which occurs elsewhere as well (see Variations 7 and 9).

Brahms, *Handel Variations*. Brahms derives substantially all the motives for his twenty-five variations from the features of the theme. For instance, the motive of the first variation derives from the bass of the first measure, doubly diminished rhythmically. Its rhythmical complement furnishes the accompaniment figure. The same three notes in triplets form the motive for the second variation. The curious derivation of the motive in Variation 16 is shown in Exs. 127*a* and *b*.

APPLICATION AND ELABORATION OF THE MOTIVE OF VARIATION

The motive of variation must accommodate itself to every movement of the harmony (which itself is subject to variation), and must contain all the principal tones of the theme. Variety within the variation requires appropriate elaboration of the motive. Additional elaborations are the consequences of such structural features as cadences, contrasts and subdivisions. This will result in variation within the variation.

Illustrations from the literature

Beethoven, *Diabelli Variations*. The contrast between the static harmony of m. 1–8 and 17–24 and the sequences of m. 9–12 and 25–28 requires great flexibility in the motives of variation. As a consequence, many are very short. Elsewhere the motive is adapted, or further varied, where the more rapid harmonic change occurs (e.g. Variations 3, 7, 8, 12, 18, 19 and 23). The sequences are varied in almost all the variations by substituting different progressions, often very far-reaching, as for instance in Variation 5. Variation 20 is harmonically fantastic; even in the post-Wagnerian epoch it would have been called 'modernistic'.

Beethoven, *15 Variations in E♭*, Op. 35. The three variations preceding the entrance of the theme are built merely as contrapuntal additions to the bass. In Variation 1 (following the theme) the motive is modified greatly (m. 5) in adaptation to the richer movement of the harmony. The motive of Variation 3 is compounded of two elements, the shifting of which deranges the phrasing. In m. 13 even the change of harmony occurs as an anticipation, on the weak beat. In many of these variations, which are written in a brilliant piano style, the specific formulation of the motive is less obligatory. The preservation of the motus admits rather remote changes. In Variation 4 the sixteenth notes begin as scale lines; but in m. 9 they are changed to broken chords, and in m. 13 the system of arpeggiation is again changed. Variation 7, a canon in the octave, is an illustration of Beethoven's Olympic wit.

There are two variations in minor. Variation 14 in $e\flat$, deviates from the original harmony only in the use of some transformations (especially the Neapolitan sixth). But the other, Variation 6, is extremely interesting. The theme, with insignificant adaptations, is harmonized almost entirely in c. Only the last two measures re-establish $E\flat$.

Beethoven, *32 Variations in c minor*. Variation 5 of the *32 Variations* is an example of development within a variation. The sixteenth-notes of the motive of variation are an 'echo' of the sixteenth-notes of Variations 1–3. This rhythmic figure determines the character of the variation. But the main feature, ˌaˌ in Ex. 125*b*, derives from the theme's m. 7–8, as demonstrated in Ex. 125*c*. The climactic development of m. 5–6 in the theme is carried out here by a concentration, three forms of the motive squeezed together. Even more compressed are the imitative repetitions in m. 7–8.

The elaboration of some motives admits various treatments. The method of using one idea in several variations, in quasi-contrapuntal inversion, occurs in Variations 1, 2 and 3. The relation is similar between Variations 10 and 11; 20 and 21. This latter pair is extended to a group of three by Variation 22, in which a simplification of the triplet figure is treated in canonic imitation. Variations 15 and 16 are practically identical, except for a slight rhythmic change.

The interchange of major and minor is a striking source of harmonic variety. But it is never carried out mechanically, by merely changing the key signature. For instance, in Variations 12, 13, 15 and 16, the I–IV of m. 3–4 is replaced by VI–II, and the approach to the cadence is also modified.

In the third measure of Variations 3 and 29 the I is replaced by a harmony whose appearance in c is difficult to understand; it is best interpreted as a passing harmony produced by the parallel movement of bass and soprano.

Brahms, *Handel Variations*, Op. 24. Brahms frequently produces new skeletons by changing the viewpoint as to which are the main features and which are subordinate. This enables him, for instance, to consider m. 7 of Variation 3 as an upbeat to the cadential subdominant of m. 8, converting the I chord into the dominant of the sub-dominant. He similarly simplifies m. 5 and 6 by omission of passing harmonies. This reduction to principal content, however, admits the contrary treatment in Variation 1— the addition of passing harmonies (m. 6) required by the imitations in the main voice.

In Variation 2 Brahms ventures a far-reaching structural change, which is then applied in Variations 5, 11 and 20, as well. Half of m. 1 is repeated in m. 2 (Ex. 127*c*), which reduces the significance of m. 2 to that of a mere interpolation between m. 1 and 3. Thus the second measure has been subordinated to the first to produce a two-measure phrase.

BUT NO MATTER HOW FAR-REACHING THE MODIFICATIONS WITHIN A VARIATION, THE PIANO STYLE REMAINS CONSISTENT.

Much of the harmonic variation in the *Handel Variations* derives from the melodic progression from the *B*♭ of the first measure to the *D* in the third. Brahms converts this into a harmonic progression by transplanting it to the bass as a root progression: tonic–mediant. Thus the mediant in the third measure in Variations 7, 9, 11, 14 and 19 is utilized to lead to cadences on the dominant, or on the mediant (major or minor). In the minor variations (5, 6 and 13) the third measures stand on mediant major (*D*♭), and the cadences lead to V, III and V. Among other interesting harmonic variations, in Variation 4 the third measure is VI, and in Variation 17 it is IV (instead of I or III).

The twentieth variation is characterized by chromatic movement in melody and bass. In the ninth variation, the B-section begins on the dominant (*F*); but the written-out repetition begins on *F*♯ (in the meaning of *G*♭), establishing the closely related region of flat submediant major.

COUNTERPOINT IN VARIATIONS

In some respects all variations have a certain relation to counterpoint, if only to the preliminary exercises: the five species—adding one or more voices to a 'cantus firmus'. In variations, the theme acts as cantus firmus; perhaps also the acceleration of the motus derives from this source.

But every sort of contrapuntal treatment may be found, and sometimes the entire organization of a variation is based upon contrapuntal procedures. Structural changes may be very far-reaching when, for instance, a fugue is built upon a derivative of the theme.

Illustrations from the literature

Beethoven, *32 Variations in c minor*. Most of the variations consist in adding one or more voices to the basic scheme. The procedure, with respect to the bass, is similar to the passacaglias of Bach and Brahms, and the ostinato finale of Brahms's *Haydn Variations*.

Of a higher order are those variations which display combinative counterpoint. Free imitations appear in Variation 17; a canon in Variation 22. Variations 10 and 11, 20 and 21 are in double counterpoint at the octave.

Beethoven, *Variations in E*♭, Op. 35. Variation 7 is canonic, and the set is concluded with a *Finale alla Fuga*.

Beethoven, *Diabelli Variations*. Contrapuntal devices include: a fugue (Variation 32) and a fughetta (Variation 24), canonic imitation in Variations 19 and 20, and free imitation in many others, e.g. 4, 11, 14, 20 and 30.

Brahms, *Handel Variations*. The Finale is again a fugue. Variation 6 is a canon;

Variation 8 is based on double counterpoint at the octave. Quasi-contrapuntal pianistic imitations contribute to the coherence within Variations 16, 18, 23 and 24.

From the viewpoint of contrapuntal artistry, Variations 4 and 8 of Brahms's *Variations on a Theme of Haydn*, Op. 56a, are of particular interest. Variation 4 consists of double, or rather triple, counterpoint, invertible at the octave and twelfth. Variation 8 contains a complex of mirror forms in multiple counterpoint.

SKETCHING THE VARIATIONS

In preparation for the composition of a set of variations, the theme should be thoroughly explored and the best openings for variations determined. After the theme has been reduced to its essentials, a large number of sketches, which explore a variety of motives of variation, should be made. Even if many of them prove stiff and awkward, or if an otherwise promising motive turns out to be unworkable, nevertheless the composer acquires an intimate acquaintance with the theme, its possibilities, and the limitations it imposes. Often elements of different sketches may be combined to provide a striking and effective motive of variation.

From the many partial sketches the more promising may then be selected for completion and polishing.

COMMENT ON EXAMPLES 126

In Ex. 126a a skeleton is derived from Beethoven's Piano Sonata, Op. 79–III. In this particular case little more than the simplified melody and the bass proves necessary. The following examples illustrate the application of a number of simple motives of variation.

In Ex. 126b the melody notes are circumscribed with appoggiaturas and intervening sixteenth-notes, which provide continuous movement. The bass is subjected only to a slight rhythmic change. In this somewhat primitive treatment the main notes always appear at the same point in the figure.

Ex. 126c achieves more fluency and variety by avoiding such mechanical reiteration; the main notes are somewhat freely distributed, though they remain in the same half-measure. A simple figuration is applied to the accompaniment. The variety in Ex. 126d, in which notes of various lengths are used, is even greater.

In Ex. 126e the bass is treated as the melodic voice and the upper elements become the accompaniment.

The accompaniment in Ex. 126d, f and g, is the object of considerable variation through rhythmic changes, use of inversions and harmonic enrichment.

Ex. 126g is carried out completely. The motive-forms are shifted and further varied in the region of the cadence. The rhythmic figure ⌐a⌐ evolves to maintain the motus, and the suspensions of the motive of variation are split into separate eighths in m. 6–7.

ORGANIZATION OF THE SET

A distinction is often made between formal variations and character variations. But there is no reason to suppose that a variation can be so formal as not to possess character. On the contrary, it is precisely the character which contributes variety. Every composer, in sketching motives for variation, will consider the necessity of providing sufficient contrast of character.

Such contrasts are especially necessary if the piece, in traditional fashion, offers no greater key contrast between variations than tonic major—tonic minor (*maggiore*—*minore*). The *Six Variations*, Op. 34, of Beethoven present a unique deviation from this principle. While the theme is in *F*, the variations are in *D, B♭, G, E♭, c, F*. There are also great differences of tempo and character. The theme and first variation are adagio; the second, 'allegro ma non troppo'; the third, allegretto; the fourth, 'tempo di Menuetto'; the fifth, 'Marcia: allegretto'; the sixth, allegretto; followed by a coda section which returns to the adagio of the beginning. The contrast of character is further enhanced by altering the metre: 2/4, 2/4, 6/8, 4/4, 3/4, 2/4, 6/8, 2/4.

From the standpoint of aesthetics, there is no reason why the whole set should be restricted to one tonic. The symphony and the sonata long ago outgrew this restriction.

Brahms increases variety by intermingling lyric variations with the more rhythmic ones. In the *Handel Variations* one might tentatively characterize some of the variations as: lyric or cantabile (5, 6 and 11); impassioned (9 and 20); rhythmic (7 and 8); Hungarian (13); musette-like (22). Note the suggestive interpretive indications: legato, staccato, risoluto, dolce, energico, grazioso, leggiero.

The most important principle of organization is variety. This does not preclude grouping two or three variations, without considerable change of character, especially if an idea is elaborated in several steps. Since Beethoven, the general tendency has been to build up toward a climax (in very long sets, a series of climaxes), which may be emotional, rhythmic, dynamic, velocitative or any combination of these.

Occasionally a short bridge or transition is inserted between variations (e.g. *Six Variations*, Op. 34, Variations 5–6). Generally, also, a coda or finale is added, which is sometimes an outgrowth of the last variation. Detailed discussion of techniques for such passages will be reserved for Chapter XVIII.

VARIATIONS

Ex. 124
a) *Beethoven*, Diabelli Variations, Op.120

b) Var. 2   c) Var. 9   d) Var. 11

Ex. 125
Beethoven, 32 Variations in C-minor
a) Var. 4

b) Var. 5   c) Theme, meas. 7

Ex.126
Beethoven, Op.79- III

Ex.127

a) *Brahms*, Händel Variations, Op.24

b) Retrograde of excerpt from a)

c) Var. 16

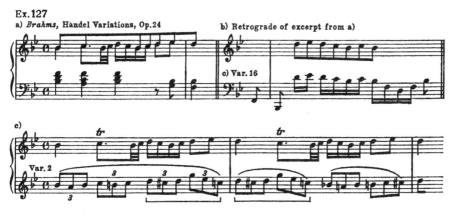

c)

Var. 2

PART III

LARGE FORMS

XVIII

THE PARTS OF LARGER FORMS (SUBSIDIARY FORMULATIONS)

LARGER forms may consist of larger parts, or more parts, or both.

Smaller parts may be expanded by means of internal repetitions, sequences, extensions, liquidations and broadening of connectives. The number of parts may be increased by supplying codettas, episodes, etc. In such situations, derivatives of the basic motive are formulated into new thematic units. Their structural function, however, is co-ordinate rather than contrasting.

Large forms develop through the generating power of contrasts. There are innumerable kinds of contrast; the larger the piece, the more types of contrast should be present to illuminate the main idea.

In the simpler forms the chief contrast is furnished by the harmony, organized to express appropriate related regions. In the scherzo the modulatory is presented in opposition to the stable. In larger forms a modulatory passage may be organized into an independent section, the TRANSITION, which connects the main theme with another stable contrasting idea, the secondary or subordinate theme.

THE TRANSITION

The purpose of a transition is not only to introduce a contrast; it is, itself, a contrast. It may begin, after the end of the main theme, with new thematic formulations; or the end of the main theme may be modified thematically and harmonically into a connecting segment.

A transition, especially if it is an independent section, belongs to the group of subsidiary ideas. Transitions appear at various places in larger forms; between principal and subordinate themes (modulating to a different region); as retransitions (returning to the tonic); or, in the recapitulation, reformulated as a roundabout way from tonic to tonic.

The structure of a transition ordinarily includes four elements: establishment of the transitional idea (through repetition, often sequential); modulation (often in several stages); liquidation of motival characteristics; and establishment of a suitable upbeat chord. These aspects may overlap in varying degrees.

THE TRANSITION WITH AN INDEPENDENT THEME

When a special transitional theme follows the main theme, it is customarily different in structure from the preceding and following themes. The theme consists of a short segment within which the constituent motive-forms are only slightly varied. Short rhythmic figures lend themselves readily and flexibly to the processes of modulation and liquidation. After the initial statement, at least a partial repetition establishes the idea, after which modulation begins. Fluid change of region and prompt elimination of characteristic features distinguish the transition from the stable themes which normally precede and follow it.

Illustrations from the literature

Op. 2/2–I. The transition starts in m. 32, with a segment of four measures, built from an inversion of m. 9–10 of the main theme. A partial repetition (a third higher) modulates to V of the dominant (m. 42). Over a pedal point the scale line is liquidated by interrupting the descent twice. M. 42–57 dwell on the dominant, a fact which facilitates the conversion of *E* major (m. 39) into *e* minor (m. 58).

Op. 2/2–IV. The initial segment of the transition is built on a cadence (m. 17–20), above which a figure in sixteenths provides the motival content. In the continuation only two measures are repeated (with a slight variation), followed by a turn toward the dominant region, *E* (m. 24), the tonic of the following section.

Op. 2/3–I. The initial segment of the transition consists of four measures (m. 13–16). Its repetition is modified to end on V (m. 21), around which the harmony dwells for six measures, still without any real modulation (the *F♯* remains merely ornamental). The relation to the following subordinate theme is peculiar (see p. 183).

Op. 10/3–IV. This very short Rondo contains all the normal constituent parts in miniature. The transition (m. 9), in spite of an internal repetition, consists of only seven measures, and leads merely to a V, without any real modulation.

Op. 7–IV. The transition starts (m. 17) with a motive, in the left hand, which previously appeared (m. 9) as the motive of the contrasting middle section of the main theme. It settles down (m. 24) to an interchange of I and V of the dominant region, associated with the usual liquidation. Surprisingly, it ends (m. 36) with an enriched cadence (starting in m. 30) to I of the dominant region. The ending on I of the dominant region cannot here be convincingly explained as an overlap. It is better explained by the fact that an ending on V would not have been a good introduction for the following ♭VI, an artificial dominant.

Op. 13–III. The initial segment of the transition (m. 18–21) consists of little more than a modulatory progression. A sequence-like repetition ends on I of the mediant region, overlapping the beginning of the subordinate theme.

Op. 31/2–II. The initial segment of the transition consists of two phrases above a pedal point on $B\flat$ (m. 18–21). In m. 22, the first phrase is repeated in such a variation that its second measure can be understood as deriving rhythmically from the second phrase. From this variant a little episode evolves, over a pedal point on V of the dominant region, which is liquidated in m. 27–30.

For additional examples of independent transitions, see also: Op. 10/1–I, m. 32; Op. 22–II, m. 13–18; Op. 90–I, m. 25.

TRANSITIONS EVOLVING FROM THE PREVIOUS THEME

Technically, it makes no essential difference whether the process of modulation and liquidation is applied to a special theme, or to elements of the main theme. Sometimes the modulation starts promptly and the transitional character is pronounced. In other cases almost the entire main theme is repeated and transitional features are postponed to the last measures. These instances make the impression of varied repetitions, the transitional techniques at the end growing out of the variation.

Illustrations from the literature

Op. 2/1–I. A transposition of the beginning of the main theme (m. 9) initiates the modulation. Liquidation begins immediately, while the harmony moves sequentially to V of the mediant region (relative major), which, at the third approach, becomes a pedal point below the subordinate theme.

Op. 2/3–IV. A direct quotation of the first four measures of the main theme is diverted harmonically by the introduction of $D\sharp$ in its final chord. The last two measures are sequenced and then liquidated by the chain-like linkage of residues in a descending scale line, leading to V of the dominant region.

Op. 14/1–I. A quotation of the beginning (m. 13) is diverted through chromatic progressions to V of the dominant (m. 17), which is firmly established over a pedal point.

The previous three examples grew out of the *beginning* of the main theme. The next two make use of its *ending*.

Op. 13–I. After an introduction, the principal theme appears in m. 11. It ends on the dominant in m. 35, with a quarter-note figure related to the initial figure. This figure—the 'tail' of the theme—is picked up and used quasi-sequentially (m. 39) to lead to V of the relative major. (Oddly, the subordinate theme lies in $e\flat$, instead of the expected $E\flat$.)

Op. 31/1–III. In each of its many repetitions the main theme ends with a twice repeated figure (cf. m. 15–16, 31–32). This figure (m. 33) supplies all the material for the transition. Observe the reduction to its upbeat (m. 36), which, in chain linkage, provides the liquidation.

Op. 7–I. Here the opening motive is joined (m. 25–28) with a rhythmically new motive-form (m. 27) to move rather abruptly to V of the dominant region (m. 35).

In some instances, instead of fragments of the main theme reorganized to produce a distant formulation, the principal theme is repeated substantially in its entirety, but adapted to modulatory harmony.

Op. 53–I. A slightly varied repetition of the beginning appears in m. 14. The continuation in m. 18 is transposed up a third, as compared to the original statement in m. 5. An inserted measure (22) on the augmented sixth chord leads to V of E. The ensuing passage work is considerably extended by way of liquidation. Thus every element of the main theme appears in the transitional section.

Op. 57–I. In m. 17 a varied repetition of the beginning occurs. The long notes of the original formulation are subdivided into an alternating chord pattern, the insertion of which stretches the content of the first four measures to six. A varied repetition of the last phrase (m. 23) is diverted to the dominant of $a\flat$ minor. The ensuing measures of liquidation permit the ear to accept it as the dominant of $A\flat$ major at the entry of the subordinate theme (m. 36).

The modification, reduction or omission of the transition in the recapitulation section are discussed on pp. 193–5.

THE RETRANSITION

In rondos, the return from the subordinate theme to the principal theme, and in sonatas, the return to the beginning after the exposition, are generally so simple that no special segment is necessary. Nevertheless, there are occasionally small connecting segments, which act as both 'bridges' and 'spacers'. See, for example, Op. 2/2–IV, m. 39–41, or m. 95–100; Op. 7–IV, m. 48–49, and m. 89–93.

Functionally and psychologically more important are the retransitions after modulatory contrasts and *Durchführungen*. Since the actual remodulation usually takes place as a part of the preceding modulatory section, the retransition proper starts on the upbeat harmony, and generally consists of little more than liquidation of the motival residues. The motive material often derives from subsidiary themes; sometimes references to features of the principal theme forecast its return.

Illustrations from the literature

Op. 2/2–I, m. 210–24, and Op. 10/1–I, m. 158–67, exhibit little more than liquidating devices around the dominant harmony.

In Op. 28–I, m. 257–68 the retransition carries out a real modulation, using motive material from the closing theme. The *Durchführung* proper comes to a close on a V of the submediant which is affirmed over a pedal point for thirty-eight measures. By contrast the real dominant is maintained for only two measures (m. 267–8).

Op. 7–I is even more extraordinary (if not unique). Remodulation plus retransition here takes place in two measures (m. 187–8), and, moreover, after dwelling for a time in the exceedingly remote regions of *a* minor and *d* minor.

Op. 2/1–I. The retransition (m. 93) differs from the first two examples only with respect to the motive material which clearly anticipates the second measure of the principal theme.

Op. 31/1–I. In m. 170 the syncopated rhythm in the right hand is a hint at one of the chief features of the theme.

Op. 90–I. A sixteenth-note figure appears on the second beat of m. 130 which, in m. 133, is augmented to longer note values. After several additional rhythmic metamorphoses, it turns out to be a preparation for the first three notes of the theme (m. 144).

Op. 53–I, m. 146. The sixteenth-note figure from m. 3, over an ostinato, serves as a preparation for the corresponding measure of the recapitulation.

Eroica Symphony–I. The retransition is a very dramatic case. It starts in m. 366, on the submediant of the tonic minor (♭VI), with the motive-form of m. 5, which is soon liquidated and reduced to a single repeated tone. It is concluded with the famous entrance of the horn, which presents the tonic form of the main theme accompanied by the sustained dominant harmony. Wagner, who was probably right, considered it a misprint, and had the horn play in B♭ instead of E♭.

Op. 13–I. The dominant is reached in m. 167 and remains as a pedal in the left hand up to m. 187. The frequent dynamic changes and *sforzati* help to make this retransition the dramatic climax of the whole movement. The phrases in m. 171–4 and 179–81 are easily recognizable anticipations of the main theme, to which the eighth-note figure beginning in m. 187 is also related. The eight-measure passage, m. 187–94, functions both as a liquidation of the stormy climax and as a connective to the beginning of the recapitulation.

Op. 10/3–IV. The entire retransition derives from the principal theme, beginning with a quotation of the opening (m. 46), which, were it not in 'the wrong key', could be mistaken for the recapitulation. It leads to the dominant region, using harmony from the tonic minor, and is followed by a liquidating passage (m. 50), derived from m. 3 of the theme.

Op. 22–IV. The C-section of this rondo ends in the tonic minor (m. 103). Further modulation would not harmonically be necessary. But perhaps a *contrast* was necessary because much of the preceding section was in or around *b♭* minor. This is provided by a turn to a rather remote region (m. 105) and a subsequent remodulation. The thematic material of these measures is practically a transposition of the main motive, which is neutralized in the continuation.

THE GROUP OF SUBORDINATE THEMES

Subordinate themes may have originated as condensations and stabilizations within a contrasting modulatory movement. At first little more than episodes, they later developed into definite subsidiary sections, establishing and ending in a related key, e.g. dominant or relative major.

Ideally, subordinate themes are derivatives of the basic motive, even though the connexion may not be readily visible. Contrast in mood, character, dynamics, rhythm, harmony, motive-forms and construction should distinguish main themes from subordinate, and subordinate themes from each other.

Aesthetically, the most important type of contrast is that of construction, since it is evidence of subordination. Repetitions within the main theme enhance memorability and, through variation, PREPARE FOR development and elaboration. In subordinate themes mere repetition and juxtaposition often REPLACE development and elaboration.

Thus there are frequently a number of distinct formulations, each established and then abandoned to make way for the next—the GROUP of subordinate themes.

Illustrations from the literature

Op. 2/1–I. In m. 21–25, a phrase appears three times. It is followed by a little segment juxtaposed in m. 26 and partially repeated in m. 31–32. In m. 33, a new concluding segment is again juxtaposed and, in turn, repeated. Codettas begin in m. 41.

Op. 2/2–I. Here the group of subordinate themes is similarly organized. The little segment in m. 59–62 is twice sequentially repeated. In m. 70 a two-measure segment derived from the end of the previous pattern is stated and also sequenced twice. In m. 76 derivatives of the principal theme are juxtaposed without any connective. A cadential segment (m. 84) and its repetition bring the subordinate section to a close in m. 92. Codettas follow.

Op. 2/2–IV. A two-measure phrase (m. 27–28) is repeated and, after a partial second repetition, liquidated by means of sequential and other repetitions of a differing segment (m. 32–39).

Op. 2/3–I. The first subordinate theme (m. 27) starts in the region of minor v, introduced by substitution for the preceding dominant of C. This relation to the transition is a peculiar case, paralleled by the first movement of the String Quartet, Op. 18/5 (m. 25), but scarcely to be found in Beethoven's later works.

A six-measure segment (m. 27–32) is repeated quasi-sequentially (m. 33–38). A different two-measure segment (m. 39–40) is juxtaposed, repeated and reduced to two one-measure variants (m. 43–44). A two-measure connective introduces another, more lyrical theme (m. 47–61), which makes interesting use of imitations and exchange between voices in the manner of double counterpoint. Other distinct formulations appear in m. 61, 69, 73. Codettas follow.

Op. 10/3–IV. The insignificance of the content (it is little more than a chromatic scale line up and down) emphasizes the subordinateness of this theme. The two-measure phrase (m. 17–18), a rhythmicized chromatic scale, is followed by a descending variation which is distinguished by deviations and deflections. A second repetition of the original phrase leads directly to the upbeat harmony.

Op. 13–III. A four-measure phrase (m. 25–28) is followed by a varied repetition (m. 29–33). A triplet figure in m. 33 leads to a cadence in m. 37. An imitative episode on the same figure is liquidated and again brought to a cadence in m. 43. Another sharply contrasted segment (m. 44) with a varied repetition gives way to a recurrence (m. 51) of the triplet figure, which in turn gives way to a remodulation.

Op. 14/1–III. The entire subordinate theme comprises eight measures (m. 22–29), a four-measure segment and its repetition.

It is evident that great diversity as to length and complexity may occur, even within the style of a single composer. The evidence suggests, if generalization can be made, a 'looser' construction, depending on immediate repetition of relatively short segments, joined to others by mere juxtaposition; and a lesser degree of internal development.

THE 'LYRIC THEME'

Under the influence of Schubert, theorists began to call the subordinate theme *Gesangsthema*, or 'lyric theme'. This was a mistake, for there exist many subordinate themes which are not lyric at all. But this nomenclature had a curious influence on the minds of composers, suggesting the creation of longer and longer lyric melodies. The lyric, or singable, character is the result of a loose construction intimately related to that of popular music. The 'looseness' consists in disregarding almost all features except the rhythmic ones, thus neglecting the profounder implications, and providing richness of content through the multiplication of themes.

Of course, lyric subordinate themes appear in the works of predecessors of Schubert, because they form one of the potential contrasts. See, for instance, Mozart, Symphony in *g*, K.V. 550–I, m. 44; String Quartet in *F*, K.V. 590–I, m. 31; Beethoven, Piano Sonatas, Op. 10/1–I, m. 56; Op. 13–I, m. 51 ff.; Op. 31/1–I, m. 66 ff.; Op. 53–I, m. 35; Op. 57–I, m. 36; String Quartet, Op. 18/4–I, m. 34.

Typical examples from Schubert include: Piano Sonata, Op. 143–I, m. 60 ff.; Sonata in *c*, op. posth.–I, m. 40; String Quartet in *d*–I, m. 61; String Quartet, Op. 163–I, m. 60 and IV, m. 46; Piano Trio in *B♭*, Op. 99–I; Piano Trio in *E♭*, Op. 100–I.

Typical examples from Brahms: String Quartet, Op. 51/2–I, m. 46; String Quintet, Op. 111–I, m. 26; Second Symphony–I, at 'C'; Third Symphony–I, fourteen measures after 'B'.

Among these examples the popular touch can readily be observed. Unified by a persistent rhythm, the intervals change freely. In Beethoven's Fifth Symphony–I, m.

63–93, there is continuous movement in quarter-notes which persists for thirty-one measures. The first phrase (four measures) is repeated twice without structural change, and followed by two more four-measure phrases plus liquidation. The simple construction is self-evident.

The piano does not lend itself readily to the song-like. Accordingly the lyric quality is not so obvious in a piano theme as, for instance, in a theme for strings. In the previously mentioned illustrations from the Beethoven sonatas, one finds that the contrast is produced by multiple repetition, unvaried or slightly varied, of relatively long phrases. In Op. 13–I, an eight-measure theme (m. 51) appears three times. Op. 31/1–I presents a four-measure phrase (in mediant major, m. 66) in which a syncopated rhythm appears three times. This phrase is repeated twice with slight variations, the second time in mediant minor.

In Op. 53–I, the lyric character ('dolce e molto legato', m. 35) is clear in spite of the piano style. Substantially the same rhythmic pattern appears seven times. In Op. 57–I, m. 36 ff., within each of the three rhythmically identical appearances of the two-measure phrase, the rhythmic motive itself appears three times. The lyric character of this theme becomes particularly evident if one compares it with the 'agitato' section following (m. 51 ff.).

THE CODA

Since many movements have no codas, it is evident that the coda must be considered as an extrinsic addition. The assumption that it serves to establish the tonality is hardly justified; it could scarcely compensate for failure to establish the tonality in the previous sections. In fact, it would be difficult to give any other reason for the addition of a coda than that the composer wants to say something more.

This may also account for the observed diversity of size and shape. In Op. 2/1–I there is only a short extension, hardly worth calling a coda. A short coda of 12 measures ends the first movement of Beethoven's String Quartet, Op. 18/6. In Op. 2/2–IV, the coda (m. 148–87) is 40 measures long; in Op. 2/3–I (m. 218–57) it is also 40 measures; in Op. 2/3–IV (m. 259–312) it is 54 measures. But in the first movement of the *Eroica* Symphony, the coda is 135 measures long—almost a fifth of the entire movement.

While an inclusive generalization is impossible, many codas conform more or less to the following description.

Usually they start with richly elaborated cadences, containing deviations leading even into rather remote regions. As the length of the segments decreases, so also the complexity of the cadences decreases. The last codettas may omit even the cadential subdominant. Interchange of V and I often gives way to mere repetitions of the tonic. The motive material is, for the most part, derived from previous themes, reformulated to conform to cadential harmony and effectively liquidated. Many codas grow out of a final repetition of the main theme, which becomes, in effect, a part of the coda.

Illustrations from the literature

Beethoven, String Quartet, Op. 18/4–I. The coda consists of four small segments. The first (m. 208) is six measures long; it quotes and liquidates cadentially the motive of the transition (m. 26). The next segment (m. 214–15) quotes and liquidates the opening phrase. The third segment (m. 216–17), a further reduction, uses only residues of the preceding phrase. The last segment carries the reduction to its logical conclusion, the repetition of the tonic chord.

Note the progressive reduction of length and content. Of course, this reduction does not occur invariably, and never with mechanical regularity.

Op. 2/2–IV. The last repetition of the main theme prepares for the coda to come with a modulatory deviation in m. 140. But the real coda section begins in m. 148 with a segment of eight measures. In m. 156 a part of this is repeated, and, through an enharmonic conversion ($d\sharp = e\flat$), leads to an episode in the Neapolitan region (m. 159). In m. 161 the motive of the trio recurs over an interchange of I and V of the Neapolitan region. The same motive provides the material for dwelling on the dominant (m. 165) and the retransition (m. 169). The next segment is a slightly ornamented repetition of the main theme, followed by four short codettas.

Op. 7–IV. Here, too, the last repetition of the rondo theme deviates strikingly, its A^1-section appearing in the Neapolitan region. The remodulation (m. 161–6) makes almost the impression of being the first part of the coda. The next segment, on a cadential harmony, is four measures long. The repetition (m. 171) is extended to six measures. Codettas follow.

Op. 13–II. The coda consists of a two-measure phrase on V–I (m. 67) and its repetition. Three one-measure phrases precede the final tonic chords. This coda section is extremely simple harmonically.

Op. 28–I. This movement is one of the longest among Beethoven's piano sonatas—461 measures. But its coda (twenty-four measures) is proportionately very short, and structurally simple. After a partial quotation of the main theme (m. 439), the last motive-form (m. 446–7) is followed by four repetitions, unvaried except as to the upbeats, which ascend climactically in broken-chord form from a^1 to d^3. The ascension is dramatically reinforced by a crescendo, and followed by liquidation reinforced by a descrescendo.

Mozart, String Quartet in *D*, K.V. 575–IV. This coda (m. 200) offers an opportunity to discuss a technique characteristic of Mozart, the technique of overlapping joint, which resembles dovetailing. It is often a result of extending, for instance, a segment of four measures to five, or even six. It is evident that the six measures of Ex. 128a (see below) could easily be brought to a definite end in the fourth measure (Ex. 128b and, instead of overlapping, the repetition could begin a measure later. But Mozart's economical mind compensates for the extension by entering one measure early with the repetition.

In this coda all the six segments overlap. The second segment starts in m. 205, in which the first segment ends. It is a repetition, extended to eight measures, or rather nine, structurally and functionally, though the completion of the cadence is omitted in viola and 'cello. Similarly the next segment (m. 213–19) is structurally seven measures, as its varied repetition (m. 219–25) proves. The last two segments (m. 225–7, 227–9) are three measures each.

Ex. 128

Mozart, String Quartet K.V. 575-IV

Op. 57–I. The coda starts in m. 239 with a partial quotation of the subordinate theme, with an expressive deviation in m. 243 to the g♭. The segment, m. 243–5, is repeated in m. 246–8. Its end in m. 249 overlaps the beginning of the next segment of three measures, itself repeated in m. 252–4. There follow in m. 255–6 two repetitions of the ending of the previous phrase. Thus the length of the elements decreases (6, 4, , 3, 1, 1) throughout a dramatic crescendo. Six measures of tonic harmony follow m. 257–62), diminishing to *ppp*, dying away upon a reminiscence of the principal hythm.

Mozart, String Quartet in *C*, K.V. 465–I. The first eight measures after the double ar (m. 227) are the result of the retransition beginning in m. 220, which leads to the ubdominant region, in preparation for the repetition of the elaboration (m. 107). This opening segment of the coda re-establishes the tonic region and liquidates its own motival obligations before giving way to the juxtaposition of the next segment (m. 235). Two three-measure and two two-measure segments follow, and the customary repetitions of the tonic.

The coda of a set of variations need not differ from the coda of any other type of movement. But since classical variations seldom contain greater harmonic contrast than *maggiore—minore*, the coda usually contains more striking harmonic contrasts and modulatory deviations.

Beethoven, String Quartet, Op. 18/5–III. The coda section starts (m. 98), after a deceptive progression, on the flat submediant ($B\flat$). It consists of a number of segments which elaborate in combination the first two phrases of the theme. In other respects it does not differ from the cases previously described.

Mozart, String Quartet in d, K.V. 421–IV. The coda begins (m. 113) with a substantially unvaried quotation of the first eight measures of the theme. To describe all the miraculous subtleties of this coda would take pages. The numerous small segments which follow are, for the most part, contrapuntal additions to the prevailing rhythmic figure. Occasional insertions and shifts cause the length of the segments to vary, producing typical Mozartean irregularity.

Mozart, String Quartet in A, K.V. 464–III, Andante.[1] The coda of these variations starts with a pedal using the rhythm which gave this movement the nickname 'Drum Variations'. It consists of a number of segments, one of which is a condensed quotation of the theme (compare m. 164 with m. 1; m. 169 with m. 6 and 14). The segment beginning in m. 174 is derived, not from the theme itself, but from the fifth variation (m. 115 ff.).

Among Beethoven's three largest sets of piano variations, the $E\flat$ has a fugal finale. The coda of the c *Variations* is attached to the end of the thirty-second variation. It contains no modulation; but it incorporates an additional variation, extended to ten measures (m. 19–28), and is concluded with a few codettas. The coda of the *Diabelli Variations*, which is also attached to the last variation, does not differ from the codas previously described.

Beethoven, *Twelve Variations in A*. The coda comprises about a third of the whole work, and is very rich in the number and remoteness of the modulations. At one point it even reaches a region which must be described as the 'mediant major of the dominant', on $A\flat$.

Beethoven, *Twelve Variations 'über die* (!) *Menuett* (in 4/4) *à la Vigano'*. This coda also modulates to a remote point, the supertonic major (D).

Beethoven, *Ten Variations in B$\flat$*. The coda (beginning in m. 47 of Variation 10) contains much passage work. There are two partial variations in the tonic region (m.

[1] The Philharmonia score prints this movement as the third; but this is questionable, for in the Peters Edition, it appears as the fourth. Probably it should be the second.

103, 119), two episodes in submediant (m. 47) and Neapolitan (m. 146) regions. Codettas (Tempo I) complete the reduction and liquidation.

The preceding analyses have shown the great diversity of formal possibilities. A number of features are common to most of them. Seldom is a theme established with the self-sufficiency and independence of a main theme. Varied quotations of previous themes are often condensed into small segments, and connected by modulatory passages, which themselves may consist of previous material. When, after a modulatory contrast, the tonic region is re-established, a longer segment usually follows. Finally, a number of codettas appear, becoming shorter and shorter, the content progressively reduced to a mere V–I, or even to a repetition of I.

XIX

THE RONDO FORMS

THE rondo forms are characterized by the repetition of one or more themes, separated by intervening contrasts.

The ternary form, minuet–trio–minuet, and scherzo–trio–scherzo are prototypes of this kind of organization. These are ABA forms, in which the parts themselves may be *aba* forms. A similarity to the larger rondos can be seen in Beethoven's Fourth and Seventh Symphonies, where a double repetition of the scherzo produces an ABABA form. Schumann, by adding a second trio (in, for instance, the Scherzos of the First and Second Symphonies, the String Quartet in *a*, and the Piano Quintet), produces the form ABACA.

Illustrations of the following types of organization can be found in the literature:

The Andante forms (ABA and ABAB).[1]
The smaller Rondo forms (ABABA and ABACA).
The large Rondo form (ABA–C–ABA), which includes a Trio (C).
The Sonata Rondo[2] (ABA–C^1–ABA), with *Durchführung* (C^1).
The Great Sonata Rondo (ABA–CC^1–ABA), containing both Trio and *Durchführung*.

The structural elements of these forms can be simple and short, or compound and long. There are transitions, codettas, episodes, etc., as described in the preceding chapter. Each of the larger parts may consist of several segments. The classification of the form is based on the number and position of the parts, not on the actual length of the piece.

Repetitions of the A-section are almost exclusively in the tonic region; they may be considerably varied (see p. 193). The B-section, which initially appears in a contrasting region, is transposed, if it recurs in the recapitulation, to the tonic region, with appropriate modification of the transition (see p. 194).

THE ANDANTE FORMS (ABA AND ABAB)

Op. 2/1–II. (ABAB.) The A-section is a ternary form (m. 1–16). A transition (m. 17–22) leads to the first subordinate theme in the dominant (m. 23), followed by a second small idea (m. 28 with upbeat). The latter part of m. 31 acts as a bridge to the return of the A-section (m. 32). The omission of the transition permits the B-section to follow

---

[1] To call these 'rondos' is perhaps an exaggeration.   [2] Who introduced this useful term?

immediately (m. 48), transposed to the tonic region. Three codetta-like measures bring the movement to a close.

Op. 7–II. (ABAB.) The A-section is a ternary form (m. 1–24). A small bridging phrase connects to the B-section (m. 25), which starts in the flat submediant ($A\flat$) region and modulates through subdominant minor (f) and Neapolitan ($D\flat$) regions. In m. 37 the dominant is reached. But instead of the recapitulation, a dramatic episode intervenes, in which there is a quotation of the main theme (in the remote tonality of $B\flat$, dominant of the flat mediant, m. 42). The real recapitulation appears in m. 51; the recapitulation of B, m. 74 is reduced considerably and transposed, suppressing the modulatory tendency, to the tonic. A coda starts in m. 79.

Op. 28–II. (ABA.) Both A and B are ternary forms. The repetitions in the recapitulation are written out, with typically pianistic elaboration. A short coda quotes the leading motives of both A and B.

Op. 31/1–II. (ABA.) Although made up of only three sections, this movement is 119 measures long. The A-section is a ternary form (m. 1–16, 17–26, 27–34). The B-section (m. 36) begins in flat submediant, and reaches the dominant in m. 53, dwelling on it to introduce the recapitulation in m. 65. A coda begins in m. 99.

Op. 31/2–II. (ABAB.) A curious feature in this movement is the consistent use of a single rhythmic feature in all the transitions and retransitions (see m. 17–30, 38–42, 59–72, 81 ff.). A short coda derived from the principal theme (m. 90) follows the final retransition, which, surprisingly, is twice as long as the first.

Mozart, String Quartet in C, K.V. 465–II. (ABAB.) The theme of this Andante has little resemblance to the previously described practice forms. There is an elaborate transition, m. 13. As in the previous instance, the same motive recurs in all the transitional passages (m. 39, 58) and in the coda (m. 101).

Brahms, String Quartet, Op. 51/2–II. (ABA.) The main theme is a rather long ternary form with codettas, but no transition. Curiously, the recapitulation begins in the flat submediant region (F) and returns to the tonic only when the A^1-section of the small ternary form is reached. Such ABA forms can also be found among Brahms's piano pieces, e.g. the Intermezzo, Op. 117/1. The effect is more that of a large ternary form than of a true rondo; only the fact that the main theme is itself a small ternary, and that the A-section of it does in fact recur four times with intervening contrasts permits tentative inclusion among the rondos.

Haydn, String Quartet in d, Op. 76/2–II. (ABA.) The B-section is merely a modulatory contrast and does not include a subordinate theme. Among the predecessors of the classical school this embryonic form is frequently found.

The formal schemes under discussion can be found throughout the literature in all kinds of cyclic works: sonatas, trios, quartets and even in symphonies. They are confined to movements of slow or moderate tempo, in which more complex structures would become excessively long.

Beethoven, Seventh Symphony–II. (ABAB.) This movement is extremely long, even though the basic structure is simple, because of the many repetitions of the main theme. The full theme, including its internal repetitions, appears at the beginning no less than four times. The B-section appears both times in tonic major. In the recapitulation (m. 150) the theme appears complete only once. A fugato elaboration (m. 183) on the main motive replaces the repetitions.

OTHER SIMPLE RONDOS

The patterns ABABA and ABACA are rather infrequently used as independent forms (though they appear by analogy in the minuet with conventional repetitions—‖: A :‖: B A: ‖, which is, in fact, A–A–B–A–B–A—and in scherzos with more than one trio).

Op. 2/3–II. (ABABA.) In consequence of the numerous appearances of slightly varied forms of the basic motive, the leading theme consists of only ten measures. But the B-section is surprisingly long—thirty-two measures. It is a striking instance of 'loose formulation'. Although there are three distinct motive-forms, each repeated a number of times, the treatment is very irregular. The phrases differ in length; the motive-forms change in interval and direction; some parts start like sequences, but are not, etc. The syncopated figure in m. 19, although each half-measure is melodious, does not reveal any real continuity if played alone. Its meaning is scarcely more than embellishment of tones of the harmony, an étude-like procedure which is characteristic of loosely formulated contrasting sections. In effect, the harmony is the melody.

The recapitulation of B (m. 55), transposed as usual to the tonic, is reduced to only twelve measures, omitting entirely the sixteenth-note figure of m. 13, 16 and 17. The syncopated figure is repeated in a very free manner, indicating that the special melodic contour of the previous statement was non-obligatory. The leading theme recurs for the third time in m. 67, varied only slightly, and a short codetta follows.

Op. 13–II. (ABACA.) The leading theme consists of eight measures, repeated, with minor changes in the accompaniment, an octave higher. The subordinate theme (m. 17) is rudimentary, consisting of little more than a motive-form stated and liquidated while the harmony moves from the submediant region to the dominant. In m. 29 A returns without change, and the repetition is omitted. The second subordinate theme resembles the first in character and treatment, but is carried out more elaborately, going into the flat submediant region by enharmonic change ($E = F\flat$). The final recapitulation of A, complete with repetition, presents only a minor rhythmic variation in the accompaniment. The usual codettas follow.

Ravel, *Pavane pour une Infante Défunte.* (ABACA.) The main structure is self-evident. Each of the subordinate themes is immediately repeated with slight variations. The irregular dimensions of the sections (B is 6½ measures; C is 9½) enhance the interest of an otherwise exceedingly simple construction.

VARIATIONS AND CHANGES IN THE RECAPITULATION (PRINCIPAL THEME)

From a structural standpoint, changes in the principal theme when it recurs are not necessary. But variation for its own sake is one of the distinguishing features of higher art. In the larger forms an unchanged repetition seldom occurs.

The melodic outline and the thematic structure are usually preserved. The simplest type of variation is a change of sonority brought about by a different setting, as in Op. 13–II, m. 9–16. In Beethoven's String Quartet, Op. 18/6–II, there are six different settings of the basic segment (m. 1–4), including transposition, figuration, ornamental additions and addition of semi-contrapuntal voices.

In piano style such freedom of voice-treatment is not always possible. Accordingly, embellishments in the melody, changes of octave, subdivision of the accompaniment and enrichment of the figuration are the usual variants.

Illustrations from the literature

Op. 2/2–IV. Variations of the upbeat can be observed in m. 41, 53, 100, 104, 112 and 135. Embellishments of the melody occur in m. 43, 102, 108, 137 and elsewhere.

Op. 7–IV. The fourth appearance of the main theme (m. 143), an octave higher than the original, is varied in m. 147 by the use of unifying syncopations and inserted chromatic tones. The omission, in the first repetition of the ternary main theme (m. 51), of the A^1-section is unusual. The unexpected $B\natural$ at the end of the B-section leads prematurely to the trio. A similar surprise appearance of the $B\natural$ in m. 155 produces an abrupt modulation to the Neapolitan region, introducing the coda. Was the first $B\natural$ introduced as a preparation for the second, or did the second merely take advantage of the accidental appearance of the first? Which came first, the hen or the egg?

Op. 7–II. The beginning of the recapitulation is unchanged. In the continuation (m. 60) there are minor variations of the ornamental connectives, and interpolated figures (m. 65 ff.).

Op. 10/3–IV. The theme is varied by interpolation of imitations (m. 57 ff.) and figurations (m. 85 ff.).

Op. 22–IV. The third appearance of the theme presents a quasi-contrapuntal interchange of voices (m. 112), though the right hand is not elaborated. However, the octave figure suggests the octave tremolando in the continuation (m. 122). In the last repetition (m. 165) the melodic line is elaborated with triplets, against the duple accompaniment. Other changes are confined to ornamental variations in the approaches to cadences.

Op. 28–IV. The repetitions are varied merely through the addition of mellifluous phrases in the fifth and sixth measures.

Op. 31/2–II. The repetition (m. 43) seems at first glance to be more remotely varied than in the previous cases. However, beyond the interpolation of additional statements of the motive from m. 2, and the substitution of passage work for sustained chords in the last half, there is little change.

Brahms, Second Symphony–III. Earlier composers sometimes introduce, in the preceding retransition, anticipatory quotations of the material of a return theme (Mozart, Symphony in g minor, K.V. 550–I, m. 139–64; Beethoven String Quartet, Op. 18/6–IV, m. 105–15). These may give the impression of a recapitulation 'in the wrong key', broken off to make way for the real recapitulation.

Brahms goes further. In this movement, the principal theme is an A–B–A¹ form. In the recapitulation (m. 194), the beginning reappears in the key of F♯, a half step lower than the original G. The continuation is subtly modified to return through a chromatic third relation from the dominant of the relative minor to the original level in m. 207. In compensation for this remarkable change of region, the recapitulation remains close to the original version in other respects.

CHANGES AND ADAPTATIONS IN THE RECAPITULATION (SUBORDINATE GROUP)

Since the subordinate group is repeated only once, after a number of intervening contrasts, variation is not strictly necessary. In fact, too much variation, especially at the beginning of the subordinate theme, could easily prevent recognition. But in order to repeat the subordinate material in the tonic region the transition requires changes.

At an appropriate point the transition turns toward a different region, often the subdominant (major or minor), and continues indirectly to the upbeat chord, usually by means of sectional transpositions of the original material. In the simpler cases there are no further changes and the ensuing material is merely transposed to the tonic region, perhaps with minor ornamental variations.

In more complex examples there may be omissions, additions or complete reconstruction, though the more elaborate changes are not common in rondos.

Illustrations from the literature

Op. 2/2–IV. The transition, which originally led to I of E, is repeated unchanged except for a two-measure reduction in length and minor modification of the last measure. But the significance of the E chord becomes that of V in A (m. 123). The rhythm of the subordinate theme is modified so that the group of four descending eighth-notes comes at the end of the measure instead of at the beginning. This theme, also, is shortened slightly.

Op. 7–IV. The entire subordinate group is recapitulated without major changes, except for the necessary redirection of the transition in m. 113. The syncopated liquidating variation in m. 147 is interesting.

Op. 22–IV. The only significant change is in the transition, which starts exactly as in its first appearance. In the fifth and sixth measures (m. 134–5) an added sequence-like repetition of the two preceding measures changes the course of the modulation.

Op. 10/3–IV. The transition is modified in m. 67–68 and somewhat extended. But the theme which originally appeared in m. 17 is omitted entirely. In its place appears a modulatory section built on the basic motive.

Beethoven, String Quartet, Op. 18/6–IV. Here the transition (m. 61–76) undergoes modification from the very beginning of its reappearance in the recapitulation. The addition of accidentals in the first four measures (m. 132) prepares for transposition of the continuation up a third (instead of up the expected fourth). Only in m. 145, where two measures are added, is the shift made to lead to the dominant. The many other interesting features of this rondo (especially the treatment of the retransition, which anticipates the main theme over a pedal point) cannot be discussed at this point.

Op. 13–III. Treatment of the subordinate group in minor is more complicated, especially when the subordinate theme is in major. To repeat it in minor would change its character and diminish the contrast. Therefore, it usually recurs in tonic major and at some later point turns to the minor. But far-reaching changes often accompany such treatment.

Here the original transition (m. 18–24) completely disappears. Instead, the second half of the theme provides motive-forms for a new transitional segment (m. 129–34). The ensuing material, while retaining the original motive-forms intact, is reconstructed quite freely. Only a hint of *c* minor is heard (m. 159) in the much extended closing section (m. 154–70), which displaces entirely the original retransitional segment (m. 51–61).

Beethoven, String Quartet, Op. 18/4–IV. The original b-section (m. 17–40) is a small ternary form with internal repetitions. In the recapitulation an added bridge (m. 111–16) introduces a reconstructed b-section in the parallel major. The ternary organization disappears; after a statement and repetition of its opening the thematic material is liquidated and a long retransition using motive-forms of the principal theme appears (m. 137–62). The exposition contained sufficient contrast of tonality without transitions. But in the recapitulation these modulatory passages become essential to relieve the uninterrupted emphasis of the tonic (minor and major).

THE LARGE RONDO FORMS (ABA–C–ABA)

The large rondo forms generally express the character of the dance-song. The rate of movement is moderate or rapid, and the mood cheerful, playful or brilliant. The classical composers frequently used these forms as final movements in cyclic works (sonata, string quartet or symphony).

Occasionally the middle section (c) is comparable in size and structure to the b-section, providing an undifferentiated ABACABA (Beethoven, String Quartet, Op.

18/4–IV). Usually, however, the c-section is longer and more elaborate, resembling the trio of a scherzo or the elaboration of a sonata-allegro. Thus the whole form becomes a complex ternary structure:

$$A\text{------}B\text{------}A$$

$$\text{A--B--A------C----A--B--A}$$

The trio section is often itself ternary, and it expresses a definite contrasting key, usually somewhat more remote than that of the B-section. For example:

Section	A	B	A	C
Key	C	G	C	$\begin{cases} c \text{ (minor)} \\ a \\ A\flat \\ E\flat \\ E \\ e \end{cases}$
	c (minor)	$E\flat$	c	$\begin{cases} A\flat \\ G \\ g \end{cases}$

The character of the c-section contrasts with both the A- and B-sections. Quite often it is 'étude-like'; not infrequently it is 'contrapuntal' in the sense that the motive or theme undergoes little internal variation, but instead is placed in various combinations with itself and other material.

Illustrations from the literature

Op. 2/2–IV. The A-section is a small ternary form (m. 1–16). A transition (m. 17–26) leads to the B-section in the dominant region. This typical, loosely constructed subordinate idea is connected to the repetition of A by a two-measure bridge (m. 39–40). The trio (m. 57–99) is an étude-like ternary structure lying in the tonic minor region, with internal repetitions like those to be found in the minuet. The final repetition of the beginning of the trio (m. 88) changes into a retransition. The modifications in the recapitulation are largely ornamental. The final repetition of the A-section (m. 135) serves as the beginning of an extensive coda. Note the recurrence of the trio theme in the coda (m. 161), after a deviation into the Neapolitan region.

Op. 7–IV. This rondo is structurally similar to the previous example. The trio is étude-like, with a striking rhythmic figure offsetting the passage work. The final repetition of A is modified to introduce the coda, this time through an unexpected shift to the flat submediant region ($B = C\flat$).

Op. 10/3–IV. All parts of this rondo are relatively short and compact. Both hands participate in the étude-like character in the trio (m. 35–45), which lies in the flat submediant region. The retransition (m. 46–55) suggests the principal theme, but gives way to octave eighth-notes which are related to the octave sixteenths near the end of the trio. The embryonic subordinate idea of m. 17 disappears entirely in the recapitulation and is replaced by a modulatory passage (m. 74–83) built from the basic motive.

Op. 13–III. The trio consists (m. 79) of six versions of the first phrase, separated by a four-measure interpolation (m. 95–98) to form a small A–B–A¹. The contrapuntal interplay of the two voices is evident. In m. 99–106 the principal notes of each part successively are filled in with eighth-notes to produce a descending scale line. The end is modified to lead to the dominant of c, upon which an extended but simple retransition is built. Other structural features of this rondo were discussed on p. 195.

Op. 28–IV. The exposition and recapitulation exhibit no unusual features. The pseudo-contrapuntal B-theme is preceded by a transition and followed by a re-transition. There is no connective to introduce the trio. Instead, the first segment of the trio (m. 68–78) takes over the transition function, the previous tonic, D, becoming the dominant of the subdominant region (G). The chief content of the trio lies in the contrapuntal section (m. 79–101). The upper voice of the first four measures appears successively in upper, middle and lower voices; in the tonic, dominant and tonic minor regions (relative to G). The other voices are varied in m. 87–95 and m. 95–100. Otherwise, the treatment is similar to double counterpoint. The remainder (m. 101–13) is simply an emphasis of the dominant of d, preparatory to the return of the main theme in D (m. 114). The final repetition of the A-section is varied and extended to introduce the coda.

THE SONATA–RONDO

The sonata–rondo, with a modulatory C-section elaborating previous thematic elements, and the great sonata–rondo, which combines trio structure with the development or *Durchführung*, call for treatment like the middle section of the sonata–allegro form. This section resembles the modulatory middle section of the scherzo, but is usually more elaborately organized.[1] The exposition and recapitulation need not differ from those already discussed, though greater complexity and more far-reaching modifications may arise.

Illustrations from the literature

Op. 31/1–III. The exposition is normal. The first A-section is immediately repeated in a variation placing the main theme in the left hand (m. 17–32). The transition (m. 33–42) uses the figure from the end of the theme. The C-section begins (m. 82) with the main theme in the left hand (like m. 17–32) but in tonic minor. The continuation makes clear that this is the beginning of a modulatory process carried out with

---

[1] A full discussion of this technique is reserved for Chapter XX.

motive-forms from the main theme. It closes with a pedal point on V (m. 129) which prepares for the recapitulation. The modulatory scheme is:

Tonic minor	g	m. 83
Subdominant minor	c	m. 91
Flat submediant	E♭	m. 98
Subdominant minor	c	m. 106
Unstable		m. 114
Tonic minor	g	m. 121

The recapitulation (m. 132) presents slight variations of the setting. The transition and retransition are somewhat lengthened. The final repetition of A, which would ordinarily occur in the vicinity of m. 205, is displaced by the insertion of a passage based on the middle section of the principal theme (cf. m. 9–10). A recurs finally in m. 224, much expanded by means of rests and tempo changes.

It is difficult to determine whether all of the material between m. 205 and the end should be classified as coda. Fortunately, the musical result is not determined by conformity to analytical expectations. Ambiguity is sometimes a quality to be *recognized*, not necessarily to be explained away.

Op. 22–IV. The A-section in its various appearances is subjected to a variety of ornamental intensifications and changes of setting. The group of subordinate themes (m. 19–49) presents a number of distinct motive-forms in loose juxtaposition. The modifications in the recapitulation are worth study, particularly the treatment of the bridge (m. 41–49), which anticipates the melodic figure at the beginning of the returning principal theme. In the recapitulation this passage is enriched and intensified by the quotation of the entire first four measures, transposed to the subdominant region (m. 153). The C-section (m. 72–111) begins like a trio of the étude-like type, in the unusual region of f (minor v!). It gives way (m. 81) to a modulatory-contrapuntal group, derived from the transitional segment used to introduce both B (m. 19–22) and C (m. 68–71). This incipient *Durchführung* is followed by a return of the étude-like segment, suggesting the ordinary ternary trio structure; but the key is $b♭$ (tonic minor), thus continuing the modulatory process instead of returning to the region of the first statement, as the normal ternary procedure would demand. This C-section thus combines trio character with the procedures of the modulatory middle section, or *Durchführung*.

XX

THE SONATA–ALLEGRO

(FIRST MOVEMENT FORM)

THE concept of the SONATA implies a cycle of two or more movements of differing character. The great majority of sonatas, string quartets, symphonies and concertos since the time of Haydn utilize this structural principle. Contrast of key, tempo, metre, form and expressive character distinguish the various movements. Unity is provided by key relationships (the first and last movements use the same tonic, and intervening movements are related to this tonic) and through motival relationships, which may be clearly evident or disguised with the utmost subtlety.

Before Haydn all the movements were normally in a single tonality, sometimes alternating between major and parallel minor. The Viennese classic masters introduced more variety by using other related keys for the middle movements.

While three or four movements are normal, examples ranging from two to seven movements exist. The table on p. 200 indicates the wide variety to be found among the works of Beethoven.

In general, the first and last movements are in rapid tempo, though Op. 54 starts 'In tempo d'un Menuetto', Op. 26 begins with an 'Andante con Variazioni' and Op. 27/2 with an 'Adagio sostenuto'. A short introduction in slow tempo, followed by the customary allegro, is not uncommon. The slow last movement, 'Adagio molto' of Op. 111, is a rare exception.

Intervening movements fall generally into two types, slow and moderately fast. The slow movements vary from Allegretto or Andantino to Adagio, Largo or Grave. The moderately fast movements are ordinarily stylized dance forms, e.g. minuets or scherzos. The latter, of course, sometimes move at an exceedingly rapid pace.

Occasionally, one of the movements is a Theme with Variations: Op. 26–I; Op. 14/2–II; String Quartet, Op. 74–IV. Absence of a slow movement permits the appearance of both a minuet and a scherzo in Op. 31/3.

The last movement is frequently written in one of the rondo forms. (Variations, like Op. 109, or a Fugue, as in Op. 110, are exceptional.) But quite often the last movement, and usually the first movement, is written in the great form which is variously called 'Sonata Form', 'Sonata–Allegro', or First Movement Form.

THE SONATA–ALLEGRO

This form, like the earlier ones, is essentially a ternary structure. Its main divisions are the EXPOSITION, ELABORATION[1] and RECAPITULATION. It differs from other complex ternary forms in that the contrasting middle section (Elaboration) is devoted almost

Relation of Movements—Beethoven Sonatas and String Quartets

SONATAS

Op. 2/1	Allegro f—2/2	Adagio F—3/4	Menuetto f—3/4	Prestissimo f—2/2	
Op. 2/3	Allegro con brio C—4/4	Adagio E—2/4	Scherzo C—3/4	Allegro assai C—6/8	
Op. 10/1	Allegro molto c—3/4	Adagio molto Ab—2/4	Prestissimo c—2/2		
Op. 14/2	Allegro G—2/4	Andante C—2/2	Scherzo G—3/8		
Op. 111	Maestoso–Allegro c—4/4	Arietta C—9/16			

STRING QUARTETS

Op. 59/1	Allegro F—4/4	Allegretto Bb—3/8	Adagio f—2/4	Allegro F—2/4	
Op. 132	Assai sostenuto- Allegro a—2/2	Allegro ma non tanto A—3/4	Molto adagio (Lydian Mode) 4/4	Alla marcia, assai vivace A—4/4	Allegro appas- sionato a—3/4
Op. 130	Adagio, ma non troppo—Allegro Bb—3/4	Presto bb—2/2	Allegro assai G—3/8	Adagio molto espressivo Eb—3/4	Finale–Allegro Bb—2/4

Andante con moto
ma non troppo
Db—4/4

Op. 131	Adagio c#—2/2	Allegro molto vivace D—6/8	Allegro moderato Trans.— 4/4	Presto E—2/2	Adagio g#—3/4	Allegro c#—2/2

Andante
A—2/4

exclusively to the working out of the rich variety of thematic material 'exposed' in the first division. Its greatest merit, which enabled it to hold a commanding position over a period of 150 years, is its extraordinary flexibility in accommodating the widest variety of musical ideas, long or short, many or few, active or passive, in almost any combination. The internal details may be subjected to almost any mutation without disturbing the aesthetic validity of the structure as a whole.

---

[1] The customary term, 'development', for this section, is a misnomer. It suggests germination and growth which rarely occur. The thematic elaboration and modulatory 'working out' (*Durchführung*) produce some variation, and place the musical elements in different contexts, but seldom lead to the 'development' of anything new.

The diagram below indicates the basic relationships of the form and some of its possible ramifications.

It is assumed that the sonata–allegro is a very extended and complex form. This is not necessarily true. The so-called SONATINA does not differ essentially from those sonata–allegros in which the minimum number of parts is used, and each is very small; e.g. Op. 14/1, Op. 49/1, Op. 78, Op. 79. The length may vary between 100 measures

Structural Relations—Sonata-Allegro

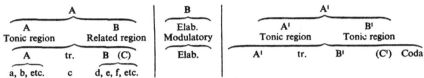

and 300 or more; only the imagination of the composer determines whether the piece will be short or long. There may be the most complete diversity in the relative lengths of the elements of the form.

While the *Durchführung* is usually considered the most characteristic feature, in many important works it is short and sketchlike. While one expects this section to be devoted to development only of the most important themes from the first division, sometimes the elaboration deals with themes which were unimportant or subordinate at their first appearance; and occasionally an idea appears which, though deriving from the basic material, never appeared before as formulated. Varied as the specific cases may be, the formal purpose of this section is, as with other contrasting middle sections, to provide a RELATED CONTRAST.

The elaboration is ESSENTIALLY MODULATORY, and for very good reasons. As the form developed the first division became longer, composed of a greater number of parts; more means of contrasting and joining them were used; more ways of building and limiting themes became necessary; a unifying restriction of the harmony became advisable to preserve the stability of the themes in spite of the internal harmonic variety. Thus in the exposition, though some parts modulate and others express a (related) contrasting tonality, apart from transitions, everything stands solidly within the region of a definite tonality. In other words, the harmony is essentially stable.

This requires a different kind of contrast in the elaboration.

Economy dictates the use of previously 'exposed' thematic material (a wealth of differing ideas is presented in the first division). Variety requires roving, modulating harmony as a contrast to the generally stable nature of the exposition.

THE EXPOSITION

The exposition resembles the first division of the larger rondos in several respects. The statements of the principal and subordinate themes are in contrasting but related tonalities. A transition connects them in all but the simplest cases. A distinct contrast of character helps to distinguish the various themes, though analysis will demonstrate their inter-connexion through common use of basic motive-features.

It differs from the rondos in that the principal theme is not repeated prior to the elaboration, and there is no return to the principal key. Instead, a closing section, still in a contrasting region, completes the exposition. Often this is a mere group of codettas. Occasionally, a formulation derived from the principal theme provides the material (String Quartet, Op. 18/1-I, m. 72; Op. 18/6-I, m. 80; Mozart, Symphony in g, K.V. 550-I, m. 66). But generally a special theme, adapted to cadential harmonies, is introduced, which may be reminiscent of any of the preceding themes, or quite distinct.

THE PRINCIPAL THEME (OR GROUP)

The structure may vary widely—from a straightforward period or sentence, through something resembling a ternary form, to a group of distinct themes joined in the most subtle fashion. Often a return to the A-theme merges into a transition.

The ideas of the principal group are nearly always more thematic than melodic (see Chapter XI) and the internal organization tends to be flexible and irregular, forecasting the metamorphoses to which the ideas will later be subjected. If the structure is too symmetrical, subsequent freedom of articulation may be impeded. A striking, motto-like beginning is a useful feature (Op. 2/2-I, Op. 7-I, Op. 10/1-I, Op. 10/2-I, Op. 22-I, String Quartet, Op. 95-I).

Illustrations from the literature

Op. 2/1-I. The theme, a simple sentence, is eight measures long. A transposition of it provides material for a short transition which is quickly liquidated, and the subordinate theme follows in m. 21.

Op. 2/2-I. There are two distinct ideas here: the motto-like beginning built from descending broken chords, and the more lyrical continuation (m. 9). Both elements are repeated in shortened form (m. 21) and brought to a definite cadence in m. 32. The free articulation of phrases of varying lengths within the thirty-two measures places the chief internal cadence (to the dominant) in m. 20.

Op. 7-I. After the motto-like beginning (m. 1-4), a series of two-measure phrases extend to m. 13, where an overlapping varied repetition further extends the passage to m. 17. But here, still further extension takes place through a partially liquidated continuation of the eighth-note passage work, which suggests a close in m. 25. However, a varied repetition of the opening motto inaugurates the transition.

Op. 10/1-I. The initial segment (m. 1-4) contains two sharply contrasted characteristics. The tonic form is immediately followed by a dominant form. The linkage in m. 4-5 and 8-9 is so intimate that the phrase endings almost disappear. The two-measure phrase which is repeated and liquidated in the ensuing eight measures is again a distinct, though related, motive-form. Several cadential additions lead to a derivative of the first two measures, which appears three times, leading to a cadence in m. 30.

Op. 10/2-I. The twelve-measure theme consists of three segments very rich in motive-forms. The repetition of the beginning in m. 13 leads at once to the dominant of iii, in lieu of a transition.

Op. 10/3-I. The ten-measure sentence contains two elements: m. 1–4 and m. 5–10. These are repeated in reverse order, with slight variations, at the end of the theme leading to V of vi, in lieu of a transition.

Op. 14/1-I. Though short (twelve measures), this theme may be considered a prototype of the 'group' of themes. Four distinct motive formulations appear in succession.

Op. 28-I. This thirty-nine-measure theme (above a tonic pedal point momentarily interrupted in m. 26 and 34) begins with a ten-measure theme, which is immediately repeated an octave higher. The continuation, m. 21–28, resembles the consequent of a period in its relationship to the opening. It, too, is repeated, and extended by a varied repetition of the cadence. The variations and their articulation are subtle but not far-reaching.

Even these few examples suggest the great variety of themes: the free articulation, the irregularity in the length of segments, the number of distinct motive formulations, the presence or absence of internal repetitions, the range of connective possibilities with what follows (sometimes definite isolation by means of strong cadences followed by codettas, sometimes complete merger without any break).

A feeling for the full flexibility of the form can only be gained by thorough study of a great many examples from many composers.

THE TRANSITION

No special discussion of this feature is necessary. A considerable number of characteristic examples have been discussed in Chapter XVIII.

Occasionally there is no independent transition (Op. 10/2 and Op. 10/3). But a well-developed modulatory passage between the principal and subordinate themes becomes a valuable source of contrast in the recapitulation.

Both the transformation of the main theme into a transition, and the transition with an independent theme are equally useful, the choice depending in part on the amount of internal repetition incorporated in the principal theme.

Obviously, in very extended works (symphonies, concertos), the transition may require more than one theme.

The more extended transitions normally close, of course, with liquidation and emphasis of a suitable upbeat chord or region.

THE SUBORDINATE GROUP

The construction of this group was discussed in considerable detail in Chapter XVIII. The most important single factor is CONTRAST with the principal group: a different key or region, contrasting motive-forms, distinct rhythmic characteristics and different types of thematic construction and articulation. There are nearly always enough differentiated ideas here to justify the term 'group'.

Some, at least, of the following features can be expected:

LOOSE STRUCTURE: direct and immediate repetition of segments, juxtaposition of contrasting segments, often with an overlap; little or no recurrence of earlier features within the section.

SPINNING OUT: derivation of succeeding motive-forms from preceding ones, leading to sequences, condensation and liquidation. Chain-like interconnexion.

EVASION OF DEFINITE CADENCES until the end of the whole exposition. This device contributes to the harmonic momentum, and helps to join remotely related motive material. Incidental modulation may derive from this technique, without disturbing the essential stability.

CODETTAS, or even a definite CLOSING THEME, at the end of the group, marking the end of the exposition.

KEY RELATIONSHIPS are substantially the same as in contrasting middle sections for the simpler forms. When the principal theme is MAJOR, the subordinate group nearly always lies in the key of V. Sometimes the interchangeability of parallel major and minor permits the appearance of part or all of the subordinate group in the key of v (minor), with the exception of codettas (e.g. Op. 2/2–I, Op. 2/3–I).

In MINOR, the preferred keys arc III (relative major) and v (minor). Since a theme which first appears in a major key does not always work satisfactorily in minor, and since the minor–major contrast between principal and subordinate themes may be essential, considerable modification of the subordinate group may appear in the recapitulation (e.g. Op. 10/1–I, Op. 13–I).

Of course, departures from these relationships can be found, particularly in composers after Beethoven. A striking example is to be found in Brahms's Piano Quintet, Op. 34, in *f*. The chief subordinate theme is in *c♯* and recurs in the recapitulation in *f♯*. But such relationships are infrequent; and they always require masterly adaptations of the form and the material.

Illustrations from the literature

Op. 7–I. This extensive subordinate group contains six distinct sections. The first, emphasizing the dominant of *B♭* (V), consists of nine measures (m. 41–49). After a two-measure (overlapping) connective, a varied repetition follows (m. 50–59). A contrasting more lyrical theme of eight measures (m. 60–67) is repeated with an ornamental variation (m. 68) and extended to fourteen measures. A sudden harmonic diversion after the dominant pedal point introduces a surprising major 6/4 chord of C. A third idea evolves over a pedal point on G; a momentary cadence to C in the eighth measure is extended to return to B♭ in m. 93. Here an overlapping fourth theme appears in octaves; it is repeated in m. 101, the incidental sixteenth-notes of m. 97 now overrunning the entire statement. A long tonic pedal point underlies the fifth section (m. 111–27). A striking syncopation contrasts with the liquid sixteenths to introduce the codetta (m. 127–36). From m. 82 to the end each cadence overlaps the beginning of the ensuing section, thus intimately linking the contrasting formulations and maintaining momentum.

Op. 10/1–I. The subordinate group begins (m. 56) with a lyrical phrase of four measures which is immediately repeated, the relation being similar to the tonic form–dominant form of the sentence. Two more four-measure phrases follow, forming a varied repetition, in which the broken chords of m. 56–57 and 60–61 are replaced with long scale lines (m. 64–65 and 68–69). A cadential extension is also repeated with variation, reaching the 6/4 in m. 86. An added segment (derived from m. 1) again reaches the 6/4 in m. 90, and finally cadences to E♭ in m. 94. The entire section from m. 72 to m. 94 is a series of approaches to the cadence. The codettas (m. 95–105) are derived from the end of the transition.

Op. 10/3–I. The subordinate group, after a principal theme which is short (twenty-two measures) and simply constructed, comprises 102 measures! The role of the section from m. 23 to m. 53 is somewhat ambiguous. It begins with a clearly formulated period of eight measures in the key of the relative minor (b). The next segment (m. 31) makes the impression of the middle section of a small ternary form. But a sequential modulation leads to A and an extended cadential process using liquidating devices definitely establishes that key in m. 53. Is this section merely a transition? Or is it the first subordinate theme, stated somewhat exceptionally in the key of vi?

Another theme appears in m. 54, whose structure resembles that of a codetta. Could this be the principal subordinate theme? After a repetition referred to the parallel minor (m. 61–66), another distinct formulation carried out an extensive modulation (much more elaborate than the alleged transition of m. 23–53), returning to A in m. 93. Three contrasted codettas follow (m. 94–105, 106–13 and 114–24), the last of which is transformed into a retransition.

Op. 28–I presents similar problems. The principal theme comprises thirty-nine measures, the subordinate group 124.

It is evident that the character, construction, complexity and length of the subordinate group are determined only by the demands of the individual composition. Contrasting but related key, character and thematic material are essential. Sufficient closing or codetta material to mark the end of the exposition clearly is the usual practice, though a kind of retransition sometimes masks the definite formal subdivision normally found. Beyond these recommendations only the composer's imagination and inventiveness can determine the events of the subordinate group.

THE ELABORATION (*Durchführung*)

It has been pointed out (pp. 200 ff.) that the elaboration is essentially a *contrasting middle section*. Because the exposition is basically stable, the elaboration tends to be modulatory. Because the exposition uses closely related keys, the elaboration usually includes more remote regions. Because the exposition 'develops' a wealth of differing themes from a basic motive, the elaboration normally makes use of variants of previously 'exposed' themes, seldom evolving new musical ideas.

The relative length of the elaboration varies widely. Examples can be found where it is approximately half as long as the exposition (e.g. first movements: Op. 2/3; Op. 10/3; Schubert, String Quartet in *d*). In some cases it is substantially equal to the exposition (first movements: Op. 2/2; Symphonies Nos. 3 and 5). The length can only be determined by the nature of the material and the imagination of the composer.

The importance and significance of this division was much overrated during the last half of the nineteenth century.

Technically, the elaboration resembles the *Durchführung* of the scherzo (Chapter XVI). It consists of a number of segments, passing systematically through a number of contrasting keys or regions. It ends with the establishment of an appropriate upbeat chord or retransition, preparing for the recapitulation.

The thematic material may be drawn from the themes of the exposition in any order. Often a small number of features, formerly inconspicuous, dominate the entire division. Some of the segments remain for a time in a single region. Some are repeated in a sequential or quasi-sequential relationship. The various sections may be strongly contrasted in rhythmic features, thematic material, structure, length and tonality. In many elaborations the earlier segments are the longer and more stable ones. In approaching the retransition, shorter and shorter segments, often accompanied by more rapid change of region, provide both a climactic condensation and a partial liquidation.

Occasional 'roving' passages, which pertain to no definite region, are interspersed among more stable passages, somewhat resembling transitions. Segments overlap freely, the end of one coinciding with the beginning of the next. As a method of maintaining musical momentum, approach chords, especially dominants, are commonly emphasized more than the tonics to which they refer. Deceptive progressions are also useful.

Movement from region to region is usually effected through the closer key relationships, though the most remote regions may be reached in the process.[1] There is a

[1] For detailed harmonic analysis of typical cases, see Schoenberg, Arnold, *Structural Functions of Harmony*, pp. 145 ff.

tendency to favour regions employing more flats or fewer sharps than the principal key of the movement, perhaps because the group of subordinate themes almost always lies on the dominant side—more sharps or fewer flats. This tendency is particularly evident in the approach to the upbeat chord or retransition.

The beginning of the elaboration may be related to the end of the exposition in the same manner as any other contrasting middle section. It may begin in the same region, even with the same harmony. Or another degree or region may be juxtaposed, with or without modulation. Tonic minor or major is quite common. Sometimes a kind of transition is interposed, or an introductory segment.

Illustrations from the literature

Op. 13–I. The structure of this elaboration is not very different from that recommended for the scherzo. After a four-measure quotation from the introduction, a six-measure segment (m. 137–42) reformulated from elements of the principal theme and the introduction is stated in *e* (relative minor of the dominant). A sequential repetition a step lower follows in m. 143. A reduced and simplified version of four measures (m. 149–52) now appears three times. Though the dominant of *c* is reached in m. 157, an extended cadential progression, liquidating most of the features of the theme, intervenes before the dominant is finally confirmed in m. 167. A long passage ensues over a pedal point on the dominant (m. 167–87), which includes two more references to the theme-form used earlier. An eighth-note descending figure (m. 187–94) acts as retransition.

Op. 28–I. Here again the structure is essentially monothematic, and based on the principle of the sequence plus progressive reduction. The retransition at the end of the exposition is diverted to the key of the subdominant (*G*), in which the principal theme is restated (m. 167–76). A slightly modified restatement in the parallel minor (*g*) gives way to a sequence of its last four measures, a fourth lower. These eight measures (m. 183–90) are repeated with the voices interchanged as in double counterpoint. A reduction to four measures (m. 199–202) appears in *d*; it is sequenced in *a*. Further reduction to two measures (m. 207–8) with a freer (liquidating) treatment of the eighths, and to one measure (m. 211 ff.) leads to a pedal point on ♯♯ (dominant of the relative minor in m. 219). Residues of the motive are reduced to a mere rhythmic reminiscence without even harmonic change (m. 240–56).

At this point the recapitulation could follow. Instead an episodic quotation of the closing theme (m. 136) in *B* and *b* leads to V of *D* in m. 266.

Op. 2/1–I. References to the principal theme appear only in the introductory measures (m. 49–54), and in the retransition (m. 95–100). The main body of the elaboration utilizes the subordinate theme and its residues in the familiar sequential manner, reaching a pedal point on V in m. 81.

Op. 2/2–I. An introductory quotation of the principal theme (m. 122) leads deceptively to the surprisingly remote region of *Ab*. An étude-like passage leads to a firm close (m. 160) in *C* (♭III). A sharply contrasted, rather lyrical section, derived from m. 9–12, now follows. Residues, rather freely articulated (m. 181–201), lead to V in m. 202, after which liquidation gradually clears the way for the recapitulation (m. 225).

Op. 2/3–I. After an introductory modulation using the closing theme (m. 91), an étude-like passage on unstable harmony gives way to a sudden quotation of the principal theme in *D* (m. 109). A pattern (m. 113–16), consisting of two sharply contrasted elements, is sequenced, following the circle of fifths, and extended to reach the usual pedal point on V (m. 129). Residues of the principal theme appearing over the pedal point anticipate its reappearance in the recapitulation (m. 139).

Op. 10/1–I. After a short introductory reference to the principal theme (m. 106–17), the remainder of the elaboration is built upon a theme which, at least in this form, is not found in the exposition, though it is certainly related to the transition theme (m. 32) and to the subordinate theme (m. 56). A masterly imagination and intuition are at work here.

Op. 10/2–I. The chief motive material of this elaboration derives from the incidental octaves at the end of the exposition (m. 65–66) and the ornamental triplet sixteenths of the principal theme. Again the composer's imagination produces a 'free fantasia' having only the most tenuous relation to the main themes. The end of the elaboration does not reach the usual dominant because of the curious recapitulation (see p. 210) which begins in *D* (submediant major).

Mozart, String Quartet, *C*, K.V. 465–I. Built entirely from the initial motive-form of the exposition (m. 23–24), this elaboration is particularly instructive with regard to the use of motival transformation. Beginning (m. 107) with an imitative dialogue between violin and viola, the first segment presents a gradual expansion of the compass of the motive, reaching a climax in m. 116. In the process the upbeat becomes a broken chord, which takes over completely in m. 117. Note the transformation of the dominant seventh on *F* into an augmented 6/5 which leads to the dominant of *a*. The next segment starts again with the motive (m. 121), and the transformation is carried further. Observe the figure of m. 122–3, in which the motive is reduced to continuous eighths with a compass of only a third. In the continuation the motive is shortened to a single measure (m. 126 ff.), the upbeat again becoming a broken chord, which is liquidated in m. 128–9. The next two segments (m. 130–6, 137–46) use only the shortened form. The dominant is reached in m. 145, and the original form of the motive recurs briefly in the formulation which appeared in m. 121, but quickly evaporates into interwoven broken chords (m. 151–4).

Mozart, String Quartet in *A*, K.V. 464–I. The motival treatment here is equally noteworthy, particularly with regard to the gradual reduction and liquidation which begins in m. 123. Mozart's harmonic subtlety is fully evident in this elaboration. The end of the retransition (m. 162) overlaps the beginning of the recapitulation. A still more striking overlap occurs in his Symphony in *g*, m. 165–6.

THE RETRANSITION

The close of the elaboration must be handled in such a manner as to neutralize modulatory momentum and liquidate motival obligations created within the section, and at the same time to prepare the listener for the return to the recapitulation. The reduction of motive-forms to minimum content, and the presence of relatively long sections stressing the dominant or some other suitable upbeat chord, have been mentioned in the foregoing analyses.

Often a bridging upbeat-like passage is inserted (e.g. Op. 2/3–I, m. 135; Op. 13–I, m. 187; Op. 14/2–I, m. 121). Since this point is the junction between two main divisions, a contrast of rhythm or dynamics, or both, and of register generally reinforces the desired contrast.

In more complex compositions the liquidating passage over a dominant pedal point is replaced with a series of segments resembling codettas, except that they repeatedly approach the upbeat chord instead of the tonic. They may include internal modulation or 'roving' harmony which, however, returns in various ways to the upbeat chord. In the *Eroica* Symphony–I, the dominant is reached in m. 338, some sixty measures before the recapitulation (m. 398). It recurs briefly in m. 354, and is finally established in m. 378 ff. A similar treatment can be found in the Fifth Symphony between m. 190 and 248.

When the recapitulation does not begin with the tonic, a different upbeat chord may be necessary, and the customary emphasis may be curtailed or omitted (e.g. Op. 10/2–I, Op. 31/3–I).

THE RECAPITULATION

As in the larger rondos, the minimum change in the recapitulation is the transposition of the subordinate group to the tonic region.

Since no modulation is necessary, one might expect the transition to disappear here. On the contrary, its effect is usually heightened, and it is often lengthened. Unless the subordinate group contains modulatory elements, the transition now provides the only contrast to the tonic region which governs the entire recapitulation and coda. Thus its value as a *contrast* becomes more significant.

A composer's artistry usually demands more than the minimum necessary changes. Variation, after all, is a merit in itself. Reductions, omissions, extensions and additions, harmonic changes and modulations, changes of register and setting, contrapuntal treatment; even reconstruction may be applied as the composer's imagination dictates. Of course, the repetition must be recognizable as such, especially where the themes enter. But the 'adventures' of the themes during the elaboration, and the functional changes due to their placement in the form, nearly always require modification.

Illustrations from the literature

Op. 2/2–I. The first nineteen measures are repeated without change (m. 225–43). The continuation, m. 20–31, is omitted, and replaced by a seven-measure segment (m. 244–50) which uses motive-forms from the preceding cadence. The transition begins to change in m. 255; from m. 258 on, it is repeated with minor changes, partly a fifth lower and partly a fourth higher. The remainder of the recapitulation is a mere transposition to the tonic key, with slight changes and adaptations of the register. There is no coda.

Op. 2/3–I. Certain odd features of the exposition contribute to the changes in the recapitulation. The transition segment, m. 13–21, provides motive-forms used also in the subordinate group, m. 61–69. The transition ends, curiously, on I of the dominant region instead of the usual upbeat chord. The contrast factor is preserved because the first section of the subordinate group lies in g (minor v).

In the recapitulation the leading theme is repeated exactly (m. 139–46), but the codettas of m. 9–12 are omitted. A new transitional segment, built from the motive-form of the preceding cadence, replaces the segment, m. 13–20, but arrives at exactly the same point (m. 21 and m. 155). The remainder of the transition is repeated without change and untransposed, arriving at V in m. 160. But the subordinate theme follows now in c, instead of g.

The subordinate group is repeated without any significant change up to m. 218. Here a sudden shift, through a deceptive progression, to the region of Ab (flat submediant) inaugurates the coda. The closing segment of the exposition (m. 85–90) is postponed to the very end of the coda.

Op. 7–I. The leading theme (m. 189) is diverted in its fifteenth measure toward the subdominant region, merging into a quite different transitional passage which is eight measures shorter than the equivalent passage in the exposition. The subordinate group recurs in the principal key (m. 221), with only superficial changes. The final closing segment is interrupted (m. 313) to make way for the coda.

Op. 10/2–I. Ambiguous relationships in the exposition may account for the curious structure of the recapitulation. The principal theme ends in m. 18, on V of iii. The ensuing section (which would ordinarily be a transition) begins stably in the key of C (V). Only its closing segment (m. 30–37) emphasizes the dominant of C. The character of this passage is that of a subordinate theme.

The recapitulation (m. 118 ff.) begins, strangely, in D (VI) with a quotation of the first twelve measures of the principal theme. The following six measures are modified to approach the dominant of F (I), like a transition built from the principal theme. But in m. 137 the second element of the principal theme (already presented in D, m. 122–9) recurs in the principal key, *F.* The ambiguous segment referred to above (m. 19–37) now appears, transposed, like any subordinate theme, to *F.* But in lieu of m. 27–29, a quite different modulatory segment of ten measures (m. 153–62) is inserted leading to *C* (V), which is now emphasized like the end of a transition, citing the remainder (m. 30–37) of the interrupted passage. The rest of the recapitulation is a repetition transposed to the tonic key without change except for two added measures (m. 187–8). There is no coda, but merely an additional repetition of the two-measure cadence at the end.

Op. 10/3–I. A similar ambiguity in the exposition produces only minor changes in this recapitulation, perhaps because of the length and large number of themes.

The beginning is repeated literally (m. 184) up to m. 197, where a new connective segment built from the end of the theme (and one measure shorter) replaces the repetition of the opening segment. The theme of m. 23, which originally appeared in *b* (vi), now recurs in *e* (ii), intact except for the omission of two measures between m. 221 and m. 225. The rest presents only minor changes up to m. 296, where an extension of the half-note theme and a reconstruction of the retransition introduce a coda containing internal modulation.

The recapitulation in minor presents special problems, particularly when the subordinate group is in major. The interchange of mode upon repetition in the principal key is not always practical; and remaining too long without relief in the minor becomes tiresome. The adaptations made to solve these problems vary widely. A few representative examples should be supplemented by further exploration.

Op. 2/1–I. The transition (m. 109) is reconstructed, using the same motive-forms, above a different harmonic skeleton. The entire subordinate group recurs in the principal key (*f*) without significant change. A short codetta is added.

Op. 10/1–I. The leading theme is repeated (m. 168–90), omitting m. 23–31, which were based on the opening motive-form. The transition (m. 191–214), substantially intact, now leads to V of *f* (iv), and the subordinate theme follows (m. 215) in *F* (IV)! Fourteen measures are repeated literally, providing contrast in major; then after a short connective, the entire passage is repeated again in *c.* The remainder presents no significant change.

Op. 13–I. The original transition is discarded in the recapitulation (m. 195 ff.). In m. 207 the end of the theme is diverted and extended leading to V of *f* (iv). The chief subordinate theme now recurs in *f*, but is soon (m. 231) diverted toward *c*. The remainder stays in the vicinity of the principal key, with, however, pervasive modifications of detail. A short coda is appended.

String Quartet, Op. 18/4–I. A quite different solution appears here. The entire subordinate group, originally in *E♭* (III), appears in the recapitulation in tonic major (*C*). The return to *c* occurs only at the second codetta (m. 199).

Mozart, String Quartet, *d*, K.V. 421–I. The entire subordinate group is recapitulated in tonic minor. Straightforward as this might appear, from the beginning of the transition (m. 84) hardly a phrase reappears in its original form. Changes of melodic line, harmony, rhythm and even structure occur everywhere. Particularly striking is the shift of phrase after phrase by a half-measure, interchanging primary and secondary accents. Yet far-reaching as the changes are, the psychological effect is only that of a variant; the recognizability of the repetition is not in the least endangered. Mozart excelled in such subtle reconstruction.

THE CODA

The function of the coda, and techniques employed in it, were discussed in Chapter XVIII. Its application to the sonata–allegro form does not differ from its use in the cases described there.

The presence or absence of a coda, its length and complexity, its character and thematic material, are subject to endless variety. Common features are: repeated cadences to the tonic; citation of previous themes; reduction in length and content of segments in approaching the end. In the more elaborate codas modulatory segments often appear as transient contrasts, returning to the tonic.

Illustrations from the literature

Op. 2/1–I. A short codetta is added (m. 148–52).

Op. 2/2–I. No additions.

Op. 2/3–I. The closing theme is interrupted (m. 218) by a deceptive progression to flat VI. Through modulatory broken chords and a cadenza, the tonic is reintroduced in m. 233, with a quotation of the leading motive. A passage reminiscent of the imitative syncopations in m. 123 ff. leads again through a rather extended cadence to the tonic in m. 252, where the broken octaves that closed the exposition recur to close the movement.

Op. 7–I. The closing codettas of the recapitulation are enriched and extended (m. 313 ff.), with a reference to the leading motive. Another segment, stressing movement from I to V, is built from the second subordinate theme (m. 324–39). A pedal point on V is reached in m. 339, over which the codetta figure recurs, treated like the end of a retransition. The tonic is reached in m. 351 and prevails to the end.

Op. 10/3–I. The exposition closes with a retransition (m. 114 ff.) which, in the recapitulation, introduces the coda (m. 299). After emphasis of the subdominant region, the dominant of flat II appears in m. 317, using the theme of m. 75. Through ambiguous and modulatory harmony, the tonic is reapproached in m. 327. References to the beginning of the leading theme and neutral passage work, associated with an ostinato repetition of the tonic, bring the movement to a close.

Mozart, Symphony, g, K.V. 550–I. The coda includes a modulatory passage (m. 280–4) and imitative, liquidated quotations of the leading motive (m. 286–92) between the two codetta figures.

CONCLUSION

The meaning of form as the organization of intelligible musical ideas, logically articulated, is particularly evident in the music cited here. It is also evident (as stated in the first chapter) that the more developed forms cannot be constructed by laying musical bricks together, or pouring musical concrete into preconceived moulds.

Only the sensitive formal feeling of the artist can determine the evolution of a motive into the fully elaborated masterpiece, stripped of excess, but fully realizing the composer's vision.

Clearly this book lays only a foundation, drawing from the practice of composers basic principles, processes and methods, which can be imaginatively applied far beyond its limits.

The continued, intimate and thorough study of musical literature is the best means of extending and clarifying these concepts.

APPENDIX

(*Editor's note*. The following description of *Fundamentals of Musical Composition* represents Schoenberg's first formulation of the aims, contents and methods of this book. It was included in a letter that he sent to Professor Douglas Moore of Columbia University on 16 April 1938.)

FUNDAMENTALS OF MUSICAL COMPOSITION

The principal aim of this textbook is:

(1) in first order, to provide for the average student of the universities, who has no special talent for composing or for music at all;

(2) to widen the horizon of the teachers (of this and other continents);

(3) to offer, at the same time, everything to the talented musician, and even to him who later might become a composer.

This will be made possible by the circumstance that every technical matter is discussed in a very fundamental way, so that, at the same time, it is both simple and thorough.

I have not decided definitely whether this will be done by printing the advice and the examples in much smaller size or by adding a 'second part' which gives 'further advice' to both the average student and the talented one. This will soon be done when I go over the whole for the first time. I incline more to the idea of this second part, because it would better restrict the part for the average student to the necessary minimum and one would not be afraid to extend the additions so that they really become of value to a future composer.

There will be discussed the usual musical forms: sentences, periods, three-part song form, menuetto, scherzo, theme with variations, the various rondo-forms and sonata.

There will be explained, and advice given (among others) for such technical details as: how to build motives, phrases, half-sentences, sentences, periods; the use of harmony as basis and backbone of all formal purposes; stable, solid forms and loose construction; transition, modulation, subsidiary themes, codettas and codas, and, especially, the elaboration. One of the most important matters: harmonic variation.

For the construction of themes and melodies advice is given by discussing how to vary motives and phrases; ways are shown how to join the various motives to build units. For variations, advice is given by showing, in a very rich manner, numerous ways of circumscribing, of figuration, of development of the rhythm and of the harmony (systematically).

There are special articles on: Manners of Accompaniment, Use of Counterpoint in the Homophony, Character and Mood, Monotony and Contrast, Coherence, Even and Uneven Structures, Climax, Melody and Theme.

A special feature of this book will be the examples and the assignments for the student.

To illustrate how this will be carried out I will mention, in place of further details, only one of these cases:

When the scherzo is discussed the student is asked either to compose by himself (according to advice) a theme, or to use a motive from a composition by a master. The example now brings a scherzo theme built with the use of a motive from an adagio by Beethoven. This is one point. And now, to build the second part—the elaboration—there follow examples of 'how to draw from one's theme'. There are given twenty different patterns (four measures each) to show: how the basic motives can be transformed; on which degree one can start and end; how the pattern can provide for the following sequence; how the harmony can behave (the sequence is added in different ways). And now follow twelve examples showing different ways of continuation after the sequence, including the liquidation of the elaborated motives and the retransition to the recapitulation.

I think this method is perhaps the most outstanding feature of the whole book, pedagogically. In my three years' contact with university students (I had to change many of my ideas which I developed within almost forty years of teaching) I have realized that the greatest difficulty for the students is to find out how they could compose without being inspired. The answer is: it is impossible. But as they have to do it, nevertheless, advice has to be given. And it seems to me the only way to help is if one shows that there are many possibilities of solving problems, not only one. This method of showing always a great number of methods of solving problems and explaining them systematically is carried out through the whole book on every point where it is necessary.

Considering the great number of subjects and, especially, of examples, one might expect that the book will become too voluminous. But it seems that it could be kept within a normal size if one uses such types which are used in new music editions and if one uses a form of paper which corresponds better to a textbook on music than used hitherto. But in no case will it surpass by very much the customary extent of books on this subject.

ARNOLD SCHOENBERG

INDEX